GETTING A LIFE – IN NORTH CYPRUS

Adrian Fleetwood

RUSTEM BOOKSHOP

Getting a Life – in North Cyprus

First Edition: *June 2006*

ISBN: 975-9944-968-013

Basım Yeri: *Trend Yayın Bas. Dağ. Rek. Org. San. Tic. Ltd. Şti. İstanbul, TR Tel: +90 212 674 92 53*

RUSTEM
Kyrenia Street 22/24
PO Box: 239, Nicosia – North Cyprus
Tel: (0392)228 35 06 - 227 24 55
Fax: (0392)227 20 89
Web Page: http:/www.rustembookshop.com
e-mail: rustemkitabevi@superonline.com

CONTENTS

CONTENTS

ACKNOWLEDGEMENTS

What follows is an account of our experiences before and after my wife and I decided to come and live in North Cyprus. We began by renting accommodation in Bellapais for what turned out to be more than two years, and then, having bought a suitable plot of land, we built our own house in a village on the eastern outskirts of Kyrenia.

We are indebted to a wide group of good friends both British and Turkish Cypriot met since living here, many of whom, together with their recollections feature in these pages. Most of them have kindly promised not to sue.

Bryan Balls, owner of the former Green Jacket Bookshop, provided me with some of the racier stories to help spice up the book somewhat.

My special thanks are due to Lavinia Neville Smith, one of the leading guides in North Cyprus, who was the first to read the original manuscript and offer helpful advice.

I am indebted also to David Potter, a gifted linguist and expert in the English language, who proof-read the manuscript. The final version was read by the ever helpful Kate Fellows. Any errors that do remain are due entirely to me.

I am most grateful to Jean Clark for providing the lovely illustrations that grace these pages. Jean owns the copyright for all her pictures.

Finally, I thank my wife, Meryl, for her support and good humour while the book was being written, on and off, over a period of eighteen months.

Adrian Fleetwood
Ozanköy
Kyrenia
December 2005

CHAPTER I
THE PROLOGUE

Once we meet visitors to the northern part of Cyprus who suspect that my wife and I live here, they usually ask three questions in the following order. Do you live in Cyprus permanently? How long is it since you arrived? And, 'Why North Cyprus?'

The answer to that last question is what this book is all about.

For me, writing a book is like starting a jig-saw puzzle: you tip out all the pieces from your mind and begin assembling them into some sort of coherent picture. In our case, our affair with Cyprus began in 1986.

Early that year, my firm had put us into the London suburb of Croydon, when the division for which I worked was moved up from the south coastal town of Hastings in East Sussex. We bought a pleasant flat in a small development towards the south of the centre and I was thus able to walk to the office, some two miles to the north. As well as releasing the car for my wife, the much-needed exercise proved beneficial and, over time, I was able to find routes that varied slightly each day and avoid much of the noxious fumes from the huge

1

volumes of rush-hour traffic. My early morning walk took me first through a beautifully kept public park just a short distance from the flat. Within the park there was an original circular Victorian water tower, now disused but still carefully maintained. Its lichen-encrusted brickwork glowed warmly in the sun on a fine morning or late afternoon and its crenellations and stair-lights outlined in white stone enhanced the medieval pastiche so loved by the builders of that era.

The keepers of the park were pleasant men and conscientious in their maintenance of the lawns and flower beds. After a particularly savage drought one summer, I passed through on a Monday morning in the early autumn following a very rainy weekend and was amazed and delighted to see how the grass had quickly grown green again after weeks of brown stubble. When I commented on this to one of the keepers he replied, 'That illustrates perfectly the recuperative powers of Nature'. I was more impressed than ever.

After the park, I would pass the fine late Victorian buildings of the Croydon courts. In a substantial limestone panel over the impressive entrance the stonemasons had cut in fine lettering, MAGISTRATES' COURT and immediately beneath, CORONER'S COURT, fine examples of the message behind Lynn Truss's book, 'Eats, Shoots & Leaves'. Something went sadly awry, however, above a side entrance to the old hospital farther along the London Road which stated, also carved in the stone lintel, PATIENTS ENTRANCE. The pedant in me wanted to add a 'D' at the end but

2

from what I could see of the then derelict building there was nothing any longer entrancing about it.

Culture was not missing in Croydon either. The Fairfield Halls were in regular use and offered live theatre and opera, concerts, art exhibitions and the like, all of which were enthusiastically supported by those in the wide encatchment area surrounding the city.

Sometimes my route to the office would take me by East Croydon railway station, surely one of the best served in the Kingdom? On my frequent business trips to London, I found I could either run for the train already at one of the platforms or stroll down to catch the next one. Just a few miles up the line was Clapham Junction, second for connections perhaps only to Crewe?

Once one troubled to explore, Croydon and its environs had a surprising number of ancient and interesting buildings. My favourite such place was what was by then a girls' school, but had been a small palace in Tudor times. It was tucked away in a quiet backwater to the south of the Whitgift shopping centre, and the elegantly proportioned Tudor chapel featured a small, semi-closed-off gallery from which it was alleged that the first Queen Elizabeth would shyly attend Mass when she visited as a young girl. The chapel itself has a splendid oak-timbered roof with a king-post system springing from corbels in the walls, and there are many other fine Tudor rooms to be seen. Things may have changed since we left Croydon, but the school held one or two 'open days' in the summer when visitors were welcomed in to look over the place.

The Town Hall was another fine Victorian building, handsome in brick with pale limestone quoins and stringer courses, and decorated generously with bas-relief carvings in its many stone panels. As well as the Borough's offices, it housed the town's main library until the new one was built next door, and completing the structure was a lofty clock tower where the hours, halves and quarters were chimed.

Apart from these exceptions, Croydon had suffered as the guinea pig for the sixties' fashion for high-rise office blocks which abound there. Old photographs and postcards of the Victorian and Edwardian streets show just how much vanished under the developers' demolition balls to create the vast monoliths pushed up in their place today. Indeed, I read recently how the present-day civic authorities were marketing Croydon to film companies as a nearer and cheaper substitute for cities in the USA.

Fond though we became of Croydon after 13 happy years living in the small flat, we felt unwilling to spend the rest of our lives there despite the town's excellent shops and restaurants and its proximity to London. We spoke often of retirement over the latter years; what we should do and where we should go. Even the exciting news that a tram service was to be re-introduced some eighty years after the last one trundled through the Victorian streets failed to re-kindle our enthusiasm. On the contrary, this enormous project meant that great swathes of Croydon were dug up for the existing infra-structures to be moved or reinforced and protected, such as sewers, water, telephone, gas and electricity services and storm drains. Most excavations apparently needed to be twenty-foot cubes, which played havoc with the already overcrowded streets and one-way systems but were irresistible for a pedestrian gawper such as myself. Naturally, the streets where the trams were to operate also had to be excavated in order to lay the new tracks. And yes, here and there, grinning through the pared surfaces like newly-exhumed dead were the remains of the original Victorian tramlines, as though mocking those laying the new ones.

Where to go remained a puzzle. Should we even consider moving out of the United Kingdom? That was one question. Much though we love our native land, the weather, and the problems of living on a greatly reduced income are two inescapable challenges wherever one goes in the 'Sceptre'd Isle'. So we began to look at the possibilities of the European countries we liked the most, but each was gradually ruled out because of climate, language, or just politics within the EU. As many British ex-pats have found to their cost, some of the EU countries are not as friendly to in-comers as one might believe, or indeed expect. There are many hidden charges that conceal the true price of that apparent bargain in France for example, and the Spanish are clever at levying unsuspected surcharges on property owned by foreigners. Uniformity and harmony in the EC are still a long way off.

That said, my wife Meryl and I, like thousands of British holiday-makers, invariably chose to travel abroad, preferably where a little warm sun could be guaranteed after months of the usual UK weather. We were both, therefore, familiar with most European countries and had greatly enjoyed the times we'd spent in them, for work and pleasure.

CHAPTER II
FIRST VISIT TO CYPRUS

In a vague programme to widen our travel experiences, my wife and I decided to visit Cyprus for the first time in 1986. We flew to Paphos in the south of the island and spent a most agreeable two-week holiday in the area. A younger friend in the UK had told us how he and his wife had recently hired a motor scooter to tour round Israel and the idea was still fresh in my mind. I had overlooked, however, the considerable differences in our ages and some of our trips proved too ambitious.

As the alpha male in our family of two I drove the scooter with my wife on the pillion. This had for me a serious disadvantage in that my right ear was only millimetres away from my wife's mouth. She is a naturally nervous passenger, even when strapped securely within the enclosed cabin of a motor car, but wearing summer gear on an exposed two-wheeler she felt particularly vulnerable, especially as she knew I had never ventured out on one before. However, her advice was given continually and at high volume, reaching shrill crescendos when I occasionally over-cooked the odd bend or two and we merged with the scenery. Although a scary method of travel, it did mean we met many of the friendly locals, surprised in their vineyards or olive groves as we unexpectedly joined them in their labours. Once they had re-grouped, however, we were invariably welcomed warmly with that great Greek greeting, *Kopiaste,* which loosely translated means 'you are welcome to share our food and drink'.

The native Cypriots, Greek and Turkish, have a much-quoted saying which is, 'Once you have visited Cyprus you will return many times' and from what we have experienced with friends whom we first met here, it seems to prove true for a surprising number. Certainly, they are a warm and courteous people now and their welcome is open and sincere. Most of the villagers are, in the nicest sense of the description, simple folk and seem happy and content with their relaxed life. Many of them are great characters; witty and highly intelligent with ready smiles and impish humour. One often wonders how many of them earn a living, because the men, for example, love to congregate in the village coffee shops to read the daily papers, play the national game of back-gammon or cards, or simply to gossip. Not for the Cypriot the physical exertion of playing *pétanque* so loved by the French – far too energetic in the summer heat. The ladies seem to prefer the privacy of their homes as they are usually only glimpsed going to or from the nearest village shop. Often it is the children who are sent on these small errands and it is delightful to see little ones with a loaf tucked under an arm, some so obviously only three or four years old, but being able to walk safely on their own around the villages without fear of strangers. Charmingly, they seem able to recognise foreigners immediately and love calling out 'Hallo!' while waving enthusiastically as you pass by in a car.

It is easy sometimes to misunderstand the villagers' conversations. Both Greek and Turkish appear for many to be languages for shouting rather than speaking and what looks like the beginning of a nasty brawl can often prove to be a straightforward discussion about, say, ploughing a neighbour's field the following day.

I think it was at this early stage in our experience of Cyprus that we first came across the Mediterranean shrug – quite different from the Gallic gesture used in France. It involves holding the arms out at the sides of the body at about twenty-to-four, palms upwards with a facial expression registering total bewilderment. A slight, exasperated upward movement of the shoulders is permissible once all available eyes are upon the one performing this delicate manoeuvre. It is a firm favourite too with the aggrieved party in a traffic incident, especially when one has been publicly cut-up in a busy part of the road network but, for full effect in such cases, the time must be adjusted to ten-to-two.

Permanent wounds from that scooter holiday are for Meryl, tattoo-like blue bruises on the insides of her thighs from gripping the saddle like a vice for hours upon end and for me, greatly reduced hearing in my right ear. There were distinct advantages, though; once out of the built-up areas the countryside is perfumed with the scent of pine and wild herbs, all made even more intensely fragrant by the warm sun. Our occasional stops for fuel for the scooter were entertaining too. Naturally, it was very economical to run but we never seemed to have the correct money and the garages never seemed to have any change, so grapes were invariably the coin of the day, a generous bunch being pulled from a large tub handy for that purpose. These experiences apart, we liked the island well enough to go back to the area a further five times, staying in different places around the Paphos district – and hiring a car.

While staying one September, we discovered a small travel agent in the town that specialised in boat trips to Israel and, on the spur of the moment, booked a trip across. The boat sailed from the port of Limassol at night, and dinner on board was part of the tour, with the ship arriving at Haifa early the following morning. On that occasion, the country was just beginning a three-day holiday for the Jewish New Year, so the port was almost deserted when we docked. I hope I am not being unfair to the Israelis, but they are not renowned for their warm welcome to visitors, seeming to prefer taking the suspicious view of one's motives for going there. Coupled with the holiday, they were very particular about who was allowed ashore, a very worried and upset nun in her convent's dress, being just one who was denied admission to the country until the holiday was over. As 'pukka' tourists we were permitted entry and found our tour bus waiting just outside the dock area.

A delightful male guide was in charge of everything and the warmth of his welcome quickly made up for the rather taciturn immigration officials in the port area. As soon as we set off, he began his commentary. His talk, as we went along, was full of interesting information of every kind and his sheer enthusiasm for the land was highly infectious. Israel is a small country, of course, and we shortly arrived at Jerusalem in the mid morning. The old walled city now forms about one per cent of the greater Jerusalem area but, in my opinion, contains ninety-nine per cent of its fascination. It is truly a magical place and redolent of its long and wonderful religious associations. The sheer magnetism of the three great religions that have their origins there, Judaism, Islam and Christianity, is tangible and the old city is still divided into areas that correspond to them. As for Islam, it is said that Mohammed departed this earth for heaven astride his horse by leaping from the rock of the threshing floor upon which the Jewish Temple was first constructed and where the so-called Dome of the Rock was erected in the sixth century to commemorate this sacred event. This mosque is recognised by Muslims as the third most sacred site in Islam.

At every turn in the old, narrow streets, there is something of great historical significance, whether that is an old church, a hostel for pilgrims, sections of the city's ancient walls, or buildings that have parts remaining from the time of Christ; the list is endless and the place timeless. Also, there is the constant hubbub of its citizens going about their business; many are the stalls selling everything imaginable along the twisting, cobbled lanes. In the Jewish quarter excavations have revealed alleys that go back to Roman times with pavements and walls clearly discernible still. Most mystical of all is the famous Wailing Wall, the last remaining rampart that supported the platform for Solomon's Temple and as such, sacred to the Jews.

The present walls of Jerusalem date back to Ottoman times with the Turkish Sultan 'Suleiman the Magnificent' credited with building them in the 15th Century. They were aligned differently at the time of Christ, but there are still many reminders of His time there, not the least significant being the tower of the Roman Citadel to which the Devil took Christ and challenged Him to jump off, and, of course, the Garden of Gethsemane. Just to the side of the Damascus gate is the entrance to the underground quarry re-discovered barely a hundred years ago by an Englishman walking his dog, which mysteriously disappeared. On investigating the area where the dog had vanished, the huge complex was revealed, the masons' marks still clear and bright on the cut surfaces, together with thousands of marble chippings resulting from their labours. It is recorded in the Old Testament how Solomon's Temple appeared to grow out of the ground with no sound of the masons' chisels ever being heard but the quarry, situated almost immediately below the Temple platform, meant that the stone could simply be carried up to the surface as and when required by the builders.

One of the great attractions for tourists is to follow the Via Dolorosa; it is clearly marked out by special signs, and the individual Stations of the Cross are also indicated. It is quite common to come across pilgrims walking this route many of whom, as an act of humility, drag or carry a replica cross along with them as they progress. About half way along the Via, Meryl and I were quietly taking in the scene, when we noticed one such procession approaching. Standing at another corner with his wife, was a Japanese gentleman, back to the procession, camera at the ready and concentrating hard into the lens to set up a shot of the alleyway ahead of them. As we watched, one of the pilgrims carrying a cross turned the corner by them and accidentally caught the Japanese chap on the temple with the cross's spar before moving on. The pilgrim had no notion whatsoever of what had happened nor had the Japanese, or his wife. We watched, shocked initially, as his legs buckled under him and he began to stagger about. It sounds rather serious when written down, but as, when a youngster, one laughs hysterically when Ollie comes a cropper as a result of one of Stan's idiotic acts, Meryl and I got fits of the giggles. It wasn't so much that the chap was badly hurt as that he just had no idea why he suddenly felt dizzy. The guide who was with the pilgrims also witnessed the incident but as he saw Meryl and me trying to hide our mirth, he too had to withdraw out of sight to give in to laughter.

Although of barely a day's duration, the overall trip proved most interesting as we explored other areas of the tiny nation while travelling back to the boat that evening for the return trip, where we again enjoyed dinner and a good night's rest after our exertions.

Back in Cyprus, and using the tourist road map sold in the south of the island on an almost daily basis we often commented on the curious legend stretching across the whole of the northern area – 'Inaccessible, because of the Turkish Occupation', writ in a very large typeface.

So, the North was Inaccessible? Inclined to take the statement at face value, my wife and I thought little more about the matter until we began noticing small advertisements placed in the travel pages of the UK national press for holidays in North Cyprus. Like Alice in *Through the Looking Glass*, we became fascinated with the idea of visiting this forbidden land and in 1989 found ourselves arriving at the North's Ercan airport near to Nicosia, or Lefkoşa as the Turkish sector of the capital has become since the Turkish Cypriots achieved virtual independence from the Greek side.

We knew a little of the recent sad history of Cyprus and the long-standing troubles between the two different races of Greek and Turkish Cypriots. After all, had not a couple of chums been killed during their national service on the island in the 1950s, when the Greeks under Makarios and the Greek Colonel, Grivas, were trying to run the British off the island? The cemetery known as Wayne's Keep, now in the UN-controlled Buffer Zone dividing the capital and cared for by the Commonwealth War Graves' Commission, contains dozens of graves of British servicemen and women killed in Cyprus in the service of their Country. On the Sunday nearest the 11th of November, Services of Remembrance are held at Wayne's Keep, honouring the dead of those times.

The Turkish Cypriots too were murdered in their thousands during years of what should be called 'genocide' by today's standards and under the real threat of total annihilation, it was not until the Turkish intervention of 1974 that they were finally rescued and protected. At that time, almost all Greek Cypriots in the north were moved to the south and Turkish Cypriots in the south moved into the north, under UN supervision, thus imposing racial segregation but securing a lasting peace for both peoples. To this day the entire border between the two areas is protected and patrolled by the UN.

However, the Greek propaganda machine is today as well-oiled and efficient as ever and strictly one-sided. Forgotten is that although some 500,000 acres of land in the north were Greek-owned, nearly 150,000 acres in the south were originally owned by Turkish Cypriots. The Greeks complain, very publicly, how they were herded into the south and obliged to leave behind valuable property, but the same applied to the Turks who also complain bitterly about their subsequent losses. It seems too that the Greek Cypriots have a single, simple agenda; that is, to recover the north absolutely and to drive out anyone they don't approve of. Hard evidence of this is the overwhelming rejection by the Greek Cypriots of the Annan Plan in the referendum in April 2004 universally considered at the time as containing fair and reasonable proposals for a lasting settlement between the two ethnic groups.

Descending from the aircraft late one evening in October we were struck nostalgically by the familiar Cyprus heat still rising from the tarmac although it was 9.30 at night. This felt like the true Mediterranean in all its autumn glory, the air still sweet with the heady scents of the countryside despite the roar of jet engines adding their whiff of kerosene. As we walked to the terminal building, we could see armed soldiers in the shadows, matt-black automatic rifles slung across their backs. Even in this strange and forbidden land then, international standards of airport protection were being strictly observed; we found this reassuring after not knowing quite what to expect.

We passed quickly through the usual immigration and customs checks in the arrival terminal and walked out into the reception area. Our pick-up coach was soon located close by with its friendly lady representative, and once all the stragglers had been gathered in and counted the bus set off across the flat fields surrounding the airport. After about twenty minutes of heading north, it turned west and began its slow grind up towards Beşparmak, or the five-finger mountain, taking us into the Buffavento pass through the Kyrenia mountain range some 1500 feet above the plain, the divided capital city in its centre brightly lit below us. Once across the saddle the road threaded down again through empty, darkened mountains and on to the north coast road in the direction of Kyrenia.

On arriving at our hotel near to Lapithos, now Lapta, we were quickly settled in to a small studio villa, soft sounds from the sea announcing our close proximity to the beach. The black silhouette of the Kyrenia mountain range to the south, picked out against the perfectly still, luminous night sky now glowing in the light of a full

16

hunter's moon, seemed apt and fitting for the time of the year and a friendly welcome from Nature. All was quiet except for the gentle lapping of the tiny waves as they sneaked ashore and we watched entranced as now and then the moonlight caught lines of sparkling phosphorescence in the water.

On unpacking our suitcases, Meryl made a startling discovery. Her selected skirts and slacks for the holiday were still hanging in her wardrobe at home. Wailing lamentations rent the hitherto quiet nightfall but it was not long before the packing procedure carried out at home was carefully gone through and analysed. As a result the omissions proved, to Meryl's satisfaction, to be entirely my fault. To this day I have not worked out why.

The direct consequence of this disaster meant that Meryl had only a single pair of navy silk slacks with a white polka dot pattern and we were booked into the hotel for fifteen nights on a full board basis, with car-hire included. Any male readers might be surprised to learn that a lady can be seen in an outfit by strangers only once. So, far from enjoying peaceful evening meals with fine wines flowing freely, I was obliged for the sake of the marriage to track down fourteen separate restaurants in the locality where my wife could make her customary entrance without feeling everyone there would be suffering from an acute attack of *déjà vu*. I have to admit, though, the hotel offering was very much like school food both in concept and execution. Also, the other guests, mostly British couples, were seated in serried ranks opposite each other, which is definitely what the ladies don't want after having eaten in exactly that way since their last holiday. While having an opportunity to grumble about this extra expense despite the attached blame, I was secretly pleased to extend explorations to seek out gastronomic delights each evening as well as the previously-planned day trips.

We found several restaurants listed in the official guide-book current at that time, a slim, narrow publication with vivid yellow cover and sectioned according to services in the Kyrenia area. In the late '80s, North Cyprus was visibly under-developed, with the town by-pass barely lit at nights and only sparsely-stocked small stores for day-time shopping. It was surprising to realise how many foods and drinks we took for granted in the UK were unobtainable then. The restaurant fare generally available tended to be only typical Turkish mezes, followed by chicken or lamb kebabs or lamb chops. Mezes, incidentally, are a series of *hors d'oevres*; cold ones first, such as beetroot, olives, goats' cheese, chickpeas blended to make 'hummus', celery, aubergine with garlic, and similar appetisers served with fresh bread. Hot ones follow, that invariably consist of sigara börek, (Filo pastry rolled up with a cheese and spinach filling and deep-fried that looks indeed rather like a cigarette), grilled hellim (cheese) in pitta bread, and calamari rings lightly fried in batter to give a few examples. At many of the restaurants offering Turkish food, the diner will be asked what he would like to drink and whether he is staying to eat. On affirming that intention, the mezes will begin to arrive automatically with choice of the main course being offered during their consumption.

Meryl found the Turkish food rich and rather unvaried so we used the yellow guide to search out restaurants with 'foreign' offerings. To our surprise, there were several. Kyrenia could boast a Chinese restaurant in the old Turkish Quarter; in fact the very building where Sabri, Lawrence Durrell's friend, had his business in the 1950s. Although the food was indeed authentic Chinese, it was owned and operated by Turkish Cypriots. A restaurant offering French cuisine was also listed and there was a pleasing number of fish restaurants too with their menus offering choices of cipura (to my mind the taste is a cross between plaice and Dover sole), sea bream, red and grey mullet, all caught in the local seas that morning. There were also restaurants operated by young British people who had escaped the drudgery and climate of the UK and set up businesses which the government actively encouraged. Our explorations discovered many such places, our favourites being the Courtyard, operated by two British couples, and what was then called Rumours (now Efendi) newly opened and run by Andrew Radford. Andy went on to sell the restaurant and return to the UK where he became a highly-regarded set designer for TV programmes and, over time, quite famous. Happily for residents here he retired from TV, returned to the island in 2004 and took over the same restaurant again where the food is as superb as ever. Recently, Andy has added the Old Mill restaurant in the village of Ozanköy to his portfolio and turned that too into a successful English-type pub with excellent cooking.

Another favourite was the long-established Grapevine restaurant, owned by one of the best-known Turkish Cypriots, Kutlay Keco, known as 'Jimmy' among the ex-pat community. Jimmy is a most interesting character in the north and universally admired. With several friends he was one of the few who fought and survived the battles at Erenköy, a small collection of Turkish Cypriot villages in the north-west of the island, during the really difficult days of 1964. More of this epic event follows later in the book. Jimmy specialised in English food as well as providing Turkish dishes for the locals, and the restaurant is situated in a delightful old traditional Cypriot house, which was well worth a visit for the atmosphere alone. Curiously, its name has little to do with grapes, but was recognised as the place to go for the latest gossip, so one heard something 'in (on) the grapevine'.

There was, too, Duckworth House restaurant, alas no more, set just below the so-called 'English village' of Karaman to the west of Kyrenia, high up in the mountain foothills. It was opened by another English couple with a young family, Ian and Linda who both cooked traditional English food and were always amused over British holiday makers' unflagging appetites at lunchtimes or evenings for steak and kidney pies, stews, roast beef served with the inevitable Yorkshire pudding, lamb chops and chicken curry dishes – all irrespective of the searing summer temperatures. And, as at that time English cooking was a rarity, especially for lunch, visitors made every effort to track the place down after a few days once they'd tired of mezes and kebabs. Having arrived in North Cyprus with their children, Ian also set up an estate agency, still going strongly after some twenty years. In 1987, Ian leased and renovated the derelict Venetian Round Tower just off Kyrenia High Street.

Since then, Linda has turned it into a lovely and atmospheric shop with many local souvenirs for sale, as well as books, prints, and paintings by local artists.

Karmi, now renamed Karaman, was an EOKA stronghold in the struggles and used as a base to raid occasionally the Turkish Cypriot-held St. Hilarion Castle, because it was here the Turkish Cypriots controlled the main road through the mountain pass running from Kyrenia to Nicosia. Upon the arrival of the Turkish army in 1974 Karmi was cleared and partially destroyed in the fighting. For a time it was a deserted ghost village until chiefly British and German ex-pats rented the houses on a lease-hold basis in exchange for which the leaseholders would restore the properties to a habitable standard. This was agreed and today, some thirty years later, the village is beautifully kept and a showpiece of the North.

There is a marvellous story concerning the arrival of the Turkish army at the village after a bitter struggle to take it from its Greek occupiers. The adrenalin still flowing, the Turkish soldiers began to move on to the pretty Orthodox church that dominates the village. Incidentally, although the church in Cyprus follows the Greek rite, it has been autocephalous since the 5th Century and, as such, is self-governing. Very often Eoka guerrilla fighters would hide in churches or schools to await their chance to catch the troops unawares and launch sudden counter-attacks. However, in the case of Karmi, a determined and brave Belgian lady called Nadia who had lived in the village for many years had the presence of mind to realise what would happen if she did nothing. So often, churches were routinely dismantled sufficiently to ensure they could not be used in the future as terrorist hideouts. Knowing there were no Greeks inside, Nadia blocked the doorway to the church and refused to budge, despite yells and threats from the Turkish troops who were in no mood for calm reasoning and academic discussion. A tense situation quickly developed but eventually an officer with some English came up and the matter was explained to him. Once he was satisfied that the church was safe and secured, it was left alone. Today, happily, Karaman church is one of the best preserved in the North, cared for and lovingly maintained by the ex-pat residents. (PLATE 1)

During the days of that first holiday we set off to see as much of the country as possible, leaving early in the mornings to travel south, east or west and visiting the many historic sites, towns and villages. Driving about this small nation we were quickly captivated by the quiet but excellent roads, the genuine helpfulness and honesty of the locals and the breathtaking and unspoilt beauty of the varied and empty countryside. Wherever one ventured, the sea was almost always visible on one side and the line of the Kyrenia mountains on the other – it is almost impossible to get lost in this long narrow country. That said, Meryl and I became confused in a largish village on the southern side on the mountains while on one outing during our first visit. Noticing a police motorcyclist in the square and knowing how many Turkish Cypriot policemen speak English, we asked him for directions. Immediately, he beckoned to a colleague we hadn't noticed before and the pair of them lined up two abreast ahead of our car and escorted us to the main Kyrenia road. Meryl said she felt like the Queen. I believe it was earlier that same day when, close to a large

Turkish army barracks, I misinterpreted some red and white barriers placed in staggered form across the road ahead of us, and innocently took a track off to the right, expecting it to by-pass the obstacles. Hardly had we progressed fifty yards when a well-camouflaged jeep, smeared with handfuls of mud, suddenly appeared from nowhere and cut across our bows. Happily for us, the officer in charge spoke English and pointed out that we had entered prohibited territory. His three grinning troopers carried immaculate automatic rifles across their knees. Again, we were courteously escorted to the correct route past the obstacles.

The most popular destination for holiday makers is in or around Kyrenia, with its ancient and pretty horse-shoe-shaped harbour, in the middle of the north coast, and after which the beautiful Kyrenia mountain range is named; but more about these features and places later.

Having been so impressed with our first visit to the north, we returned for several more holidays and eventually, after much analysis and discussion, decided that this would be the place to try out living when I finally retired and before committing ourselves on a more permanent basis to what my brother later termed 'self-imposed exile'. Mind you, he and I frequently see things differently. A short while ago, we were discussing the motivation of young suicide bombers. Trouble is, I ventured, we are told how they are imbued with the notion that upon their arrival in heaven there will be 20 pure young virgins provided for each of them. After a slight pause, he replied; 'That's my idea of Hell'.

CHAPTER III
MODERN – DAY NORTH CYPRUS

The economy is linked to the Turkish Lira, a troubled currency if ever there was one with rampant inflation in Turkey itself and a difficult political situation, although both are much improved in more recent times. Visiting Famagusta for the first time in the early '90s, I fell into conversation with an elderly lady pharmacist. She told me how she had bought her house for 2 million Turkish Lira, admittedly many years before. At the time of our chat a bottle of beer cost quarter-of-a-million. However, in 2004 the Lira was re-valued with the 6 noughts dropped off the prime figures making things much simpler and easier to understand. So the currency is now known as Yeni Turkish Lira, 'yeni' meaning 'new'.

Ostensibly governed by a democratically elected body in Ankara, the real power in Turkey seemed in those years to rest in the hands of their very considerable army; a force of some 600,000 men under arms, a member of NATO and as such, the right flank of the organisation. Not surprisingly, the Turkish army is held in great respect throughout the world; well-trained, well-armed, highly disciplined and formidable in battle. Turkey forms a unique bastion between east and west, Islam and Christianity: indeed its most famous city, Istanbul, sits proudly astride the Bosphorus Strait, its bridges spanning the junction of Europe with Asia. The capital city of

Ankara is where the 'Father of the Nation', Kemal Atatürk, set up the country's centre of administration in the 1920s. The memory of is hallowed throughout Turkey; he is credited with stabilising the country and ensuring it became secular rather than strict Moslem. Atatürk's head appears on all the currency notes and coins, in the same way as our Queen's. Among other changes, forbad the wearing of the fez, traditional headgear for generations, in an attempt to modernise the country and its people, and today the policies and systems he initiated are still observed, with the result that Turkey leans strongly towards the West.

In the north of the island of Cyprus, there are reckoned to be 30-40,000 Turkish soldiers garrisoned, primarily to preserve the peace between the two sides and to reinforce the UN troops along the border. For security reasons, the exact number is classified by the military in true Byzantine fashion. Young male Turkish Cypriots are required to serve in the army for up to two years as part of the local contribution to support the armed forces from the mainland.

Because the intervention in 1974 was an armed conflict and at the initiative of Turkey, the Northern Cyprus state is not recognised by the outside world. One of the reasons is that the Turkish Troops remained on the island instead of re-instating the *status quo* in accordance with the terms of the Treaty of Guarantee. This lack of recognition is both a huge disadvantage and a huge benefit, depending on one's viewpoint. For many of the local Turkish Cypriots it means a stagnating economy and a low standard of living as they are unable to export locally produced food, textiles and manufactured goods, other than to Turkey.

At the outset of the division, a Turkish Cypriot called Rauf Denktaş, a London-trained lawyer, headed up the new State. A highly respected politician, even by the Greek Cypriots, Mr Denktaş had always been at the forefront of Turkish Cypriot politics. After 1974, he presided over the protection and development of the north for more than thirty years and skilfully negotiated with Turkey, Britain and the US as well as south Cyprus on all matters regarding the affairs and well-being of his fellow Turkish Cypriots. It would not be exaggerating to say that he has dedicated his whole life to the job, determined to see that the Turkish Cypriots did not lose their hard-won freedom and peace by being out-manoeuvred at the negotiating table. Eventually, in 2004 and at over 80 years of age, President Denktaş retired and handed over to President Mehmet Ali Talat, who was elected to serve after him.

Nevertheless, the long isolation of North Cyprus needs constant up-dating as, since the referenda of April 2004 when the Turkish Cypriots voted 'Yes' to the Annan Plan, and the Greek Cypriots voted 'No', world attention has brought North Cyprus under a glaring spotlight, creating enormous interest in a place surprisingly few realised existed before. In short, this focus has resulted in a huge property boom as people rushed first to see the north of the island then to buy houses and land at comparatively low prices compared with the rest of the

Mediterranean and indeed Europe. Many local families, whose grandparents quietly and contentedly planted their fields, tilled their vineyards, worked in their olive groves or harvested the carob crop, suddenly found their inherited lands worth tens of thousands of pounds almost overnight.

Grandparents ran around happily in their old cars, and still seen today in and around the main towns are British motors from the 1950s, admittedly fewer as the years progress. But since we've lived here, I can attest to seeing those Austin Cambridge saloons with pointed church-type stained-glass windows for rear lamp clusters, contemporary Morris Oxfords, the odd Hillman Minx, many Ford Cortinas and a goodly number of early Minis. One particular Mini must be fifty years old with its registration plate announcing R101, and I long to ask the owner whether he or she realises the significance of its connection with the ill-fated airship. Even these days, with all the new vehicles now flooding the roads, North Cyprus still has only two letters and three numbers on its registration plates. All these cars from the fifties, by the way, are used daily and only a few are treasured 'vintage' models kept carefully in locked garages. The local motor mechanics seem to have a natural genius for managing to keep vehicles going. If a part cannot be obtained through the usual channels, they will set about making it. They are helped with the bodywork somewhat, as in this benign climate few cars are affected by rust. The complete absence of icy roads in the mild winters means that no salt is ever needed, so old cars remain in sound condition and rust is rare. Even so, when accident repairs to bodies and paintwork are required the restorers are, in my opinion, world class.

Veteran British bicycles are still about too and greatly treasured by their owners, usually elderly. I see sit-up-and-beg Hercules and Raleigh models that old-time British police constables used to ride in the '50s, Sturmey-Archer gears click-clicking with that unmistakeable sound. Rugged chain-guards that protected uniform serge from oil remain solidly in place and bells on handlebars still ring out imperiously. The hard-sprung leather saddles have by now the antique patina of a half century's contact with trouser seats and I can almost hear the swish of the thick weather-proof cape swung by a vigilant copper who caught one scrumping from an orchard of an evening, the black metal lions' heads either side of the chain that fastened it at the neck, arcing in the fading light.

Developers and builders fell over themselves to buy up the family plots, to the extent that the dream of a new house to replace the old homestead with its earth floor, naked electric light bulbs and a colour TV in the corner and of owning an expensive and luxurious Mercedes or BMW became a reality for thousands of Turkish Cypriots. So, rather incongruously, and despite the official view of a poor economic outlook for the north, the town roads are reverberating to the throb and thrust of powerful, gleaming new motor vehicles. There is a local saying that the Cypriots have gone from donkeys to Mercedes in two generations. Indeed, it is claimed that the number of Mercedes and BMW motor cars in North Cyprus is, per capita, the highest in the world, after Germany. There is a further irony here too; the roads in many places, the small villages in particular, were measured out so that two loaded donkeys could pass freely. Now, the passage of a twenty-ton lorry, piled with building materials, is permitted about a hand's breadth clearance on either side, deep scars in some of the more exposed houses testament to the difficulties presented to the drivers. I think it fair to say that over the last three years (up to 2005), probably more houses have been built than in the previous hundred years.

As the boom continues, it is apparent that officialdom within government planning has given little thought to the needs of the country's infrastructure, resulting in increasing traffic congestion and lethal driving. In all honesty it must be recorded that local driving standards are very far from those of the UK. It is clear that many car drivers do not understand the dynamics of the vehicle they're driving and it appears that the basic rules of the road are not taught. Rights of way, indicating direction changes, safe overtaking, judging the speed of other road users, observing no entry signs, even traffic lights, are not properly respected, together culminating in all-too-regular and often fatal accidents. Young children can be seen standing in the front section of a car, faces practically pressed against the windscreen or even sitting on the driver's lap, and they too suffer terrible injuries when disaster strikes. A vehicle will suddenly detach itself from a row of parked cars without signalling and move off at speed, its driver oblivious of the dangerous confusion he or she has caused to those left in its wake. Visitors need to exercise maximum caution and practise defensive driving at all times. Never assume anything when on the North Cyprus roads!

Perhaps most ironic of all, of the vast wealth generated by the boom, little appears to find its way into the north's economy to allow funding for the things the nation really needs; electricity and water utilities, including more reservoirs, better and safer roads, storm drains, sewage management, rubbish collection and disposal, and so on. Sadly, instead of these things, we see a huge imbalance of payments, imports versus exports at a ratio of 10:1 against, as the immense cash input from abroad for property would seem to go straight out again for the purchase of more construction materials and luxury consumer durables. It is suggested that most major improvements are funded by Turkey, particularly in the case of roads, or by the EU where the main towns have been pedestrianised in key areas, streets re-tarmacked and pavements levelled.

For the tourist, however, the isolation means that North Cyprus remains for the time being the last hidden paradise in the Mediterranean Sea with no crowds as ex-pats know them, few high-rise hotels – or any other high-rise buildings for that matter. With an official total population of around 200,000, according to the last census taken in December 1996 that excluded the military, one can still drive for miles outside the large conurbations without seeing another vehicle and enjoy wonderful, uninterrupted vistas over plains and villages, across forests and valleys and, with a four-by-four vehicle, from rough but passable tracks running along the mountain saddles and foothills. Many of the pastoral scenes suddenly presenting themselves seem to be unchanged after centuries. (PLATE 2)

There is one such idyllic spot in the Kyrenia range, just past the Five-Finger Mountain, or Beşparmak, called Alevkaya which is the forestry department's main centre. The lovely winding mountain road, now tarmacked, leads east off the saddle of the Buffavento Pass and runs past the side of the Five-Finger mountain, snaking its way for five miles through what remains of the mature forest pines that survived the great fire of 1995. Just before the clearing, set out with many rustic picnic tables, can be seen on the left-hand side the broken roofs of the ruined 15th century Armenian monastery of Sourp Magar far below the main track. To the right rises a high peak known in Turkish as Kartal Dağı, meaning the place of 'slow-soaring eagles'. A little farther on is the cluster of buildings that forms the forestry headquarters, together with a pleasant café and a charming museum housing cuttings, photographs and specimens taken from all manner of trees, shrubs and plants to be found in the north of the island. On fine Sundays and other holidays, the area is a firm favourite with the locals who love to come with all generations of their families to enjoy their picnics and barbecues among the true sights and scents of the natural forest: in due season, wild hyacinths, tiny violets, ranunculus, anemones and the shy, woodland cyclamen. Stately and mature, the magnificent conifers arching overhead add architectural structure, shade and their own distinctive fragrance to this beautiful and peaceful spot.

The Climate

The climate is usually described by the Tourist Office as giving short, mild and damp winters, with long hot summers, the spring and autumn periods short also. Hmmm. Meryl and I find this generalisation a bit too glib. The benefit of renting a house for a lengthy period allows one to experience at first hand exactly how the years and the seasons progress. Challenging the official definition, our view is that the winters can be very uncomfortable indeed. Although temperatures do not drop below freezing on a regular basis, plus 1 Celsius is not that rare in the foothills above Kyrenia, and ground frost can sometimes be detected in the deeper ravines of the mountains where the winter sun fails to penetrate. Not all that rarely either, snow appears on the crests and peaks of the Kyrenia range giving much pleasure to the Cypriots and their children who rush up there and delight in making little snowmen to sit proudly on the bonnets of their cars. One of my favourite coloured postcards shows a foreground of orange trees, snow settled on the tops of the fruit, and Bellapais Abbey in the background, grey and forbidding in the winter gloom with its mantle of icing sugar. (PLATE 3)

Despite the surprising number of ravines, valleys and gullies leading off the Kyrenia mountains to the north, few if any have water in them throughout the year. Most seem to have developed over the millennia to carry away the occasional heavy downpours that occur mainly in the winter months. Severe rains, if sustained for several days, can lead to spectacular water spouts over-shooting the mountain clefts, and the deeper ravines chuckle noisily with foaming white water for up to a month as the deluge gradually descends to the nearby sea. In a country renowned for its droughts this is pure music to the ear both day and night. And, used to decades of living in the UK, I never thought I would lie abed at night delighting in the sound of rain beating down on the roof.

But there is also the cold that comes with the damp and this seems to seep into the houses, chilling one to the marrow. Log fires will warm a particular room but trips up to bed and visits to the bathroom without the benefit of central heating can be purgatory. We are always amazed at how few of our ex-pat friends even contemplate an electric blanket.

Officialdom is right though, about the long hot summers. April and May can be, and usually are, lovely months with no longer the need for heating indoors. The sun is delightfully warm after the winter chills but it cools quickly at night-time. Come June and July, the thermometer climbs in earnest with extremely hot days giving nights that can be very muggy indeed. This is where air-conditioning systems come into their own with many Brits unable to cope without them. Certainly, it is most uncomfortable to turn over in bed and find everything comes with you which is what happens under natural conditions. The worst of the humidity seems to settle around the Kyrenia area and the moist sea air trapped between the mountains and the coast is blamed for the phenomenon. Many hold to the theory that the thousands of mature trees destroyed in the disastrous mountain fire of June 1995 used to absorb much of the humidity and remark on what they see as the great difference before and after this tragic event.

Incidentally, that fire began to the west of Karaman and, fanned by strong winds from the west, became quickly out of control until it was finally stopped two days later at the Buffavento Pass. It is said that over 25 precious square miles of ancient forest were destroyed in the inferno, as well as some properties. It is pleasing to be able to report how RAF helicopters from the British base at Akrotiri in the south were deployed to help overcome the fire and to prevent its spread. They flew hundreds of sorties to scoop up water from the sea and drop it on to the flames.

However, within a short time of the blaze burning out, Turkey sent over dozens of teams of foresters from the mainland to begin re-planting the mountain chain, and two or three million saplings have since been placed. Ex-pats who were living here at that time recall how these dedicated workers erected flimsy shelters cobbled together from wood and polythene on the mountain side to give them some protection from the winter's wrath, a severe one apparently with a lot of snow, that followed the fire the summer before. Now, after some ten years, the re-emergence of an embryo forest can be discerned as one scans the mountain slopes, although experts forecast that it will take all of 400 years to replicate their original appearance.

In Lefkoşa, by contrast, at the centre of the Mesaoria Plain, summer evenings cool dramatically as the hot air quickly disperses. August marks the peak of the heat when temperatures can reach 50-plus degrees Celsius. On such days, the blinding glare and the sheer weight of parched air leaches all colour from the mountains, turning them to shimmering shapes of slag-heap grey. The sky too becomes a hazy white as the sun's furnace unleashes its ferocious energy. September and October see the return of conditions similar to the early spring with warm days and cooler nights again. Many of the trees and shrubs display a welcome second flowering at this time, roses in particular, as they revive after long weeks of pitiless roasting. November, December, January and February are undoubtedly the principal rainy months, but exactly when the rain arrives is just as random as in the UK.

Strong local winds can suddenly spring up; surprising when a TV forecast for the Mediterranean might show only one single isobar lazily encircling 100,000 square miles around the eastern sector, normally a reliable indication of high pressure and ruling out therefore any significant wind. In these instances, highly localised gales are usually what are called anabatic or katabatic winds, typical of islands and caused by wildly differing temperatures between air over the mountains and the sea. Anabatic winds spring from the sea and head up the mountains, while katabatic winds blow in the opposite direction, according to whether land or sea is hotter. Other phenomena are the winds we get from North Africa or Saudi Arabia in the spring and summer months, bringing with them thick clouds of red, grey or yellow dust according to which desert is being emptied in our direction. This too is most unpleasant and plays havoc with the eyes, swimming pools and anything else out in the open. Much more welcome in the summer are the regular gentle winds. Early morning brings cooling breezes down from the mountains that quickly sweep away the last drops of the previous day's humidity, while the afternoon sees the sea breezes picking up that bring with them the tang of salt and ozone.

Living for many years in built-up Croydon, I had forgotten what beauty lies in watching the gradual rising or setting of the sun, and the starlight too as it slowly pricks the black velvet, as well as marking the erratic phases of the moon. What is referred to as light pollution most definitely affected that part of Croydon where we lived and, as far as I was concerned, it merely got light in the morning and dark at night. In the Kyrenia area of Cyprus, according to the time of year, the sky is an ever-changing delight.

In summer, the rising sun first makes its presence known by a gradual lightening in the east, 'rosy-fingered Dawn' as Homer and the ancient Greeks called it, slowly quenching the stars and tinting the grey sky to a soft pink, then apricot, before it shoots surprisingly rapidly out of the sea, turning that from lead to fire. Once full daylight takes control, both sea and sky quickly assume their regular cobalt blue and on hazy days often merge without a clear horizon to separate them. Sunset too can bring the most magical and subtle colours into play as the fireball dies from gold to red before being quickly extinguished by its immersion in the then black water. The light affects the mountains at all times too. Whenever one looks at them they appear to be constantly changing in some subtle way. According to the position of the sun, the mountain colours alter so that early on bright winter mornings as one looks eastward along the range, the ridges that separate the ravines lie back in shades of navy, dense purple or mauve slipping forward into pale blues and silver as the eye travels westward. On sparkling spring days we see fresh bursts of vivid greens as the early flowers begin to push up and display their blossom and the wild shrubs begin to put on their new growth; the tints of autumn bring sages, soft yellows and pure gold but on wet winter mornings all is grizzly grey.

The night sky can provide unexpected surprises too. One summer evening when Meryl and I were travelling across the foothills, we were puzzled to see what appeared to be a huge well-beaten copper pan appearing dully through some olive trees ahead of us. A significant amount of time seemed to pass before we realised we were watching the stately rising of a full moon still deeply tarnished by the earth's atmosphere.

In the winter, by contrast, the earth's shift to the north brings the sun up from behind the Kyrenia mountains, delaying the arrival of dawn and, at the end of the short days, accelerating the onset of darkness. Because there is relatively little light pollution, the huge expanse of stars overhead is spectacular with all of the constellations bright and sharply defined according to their seasonal progressions across the dome of the sky. Confusingly, one can sometimes notice a star moving over at phenomenal speed but after being fooled a few times, we gradually realised these were in fact man-made satellites. It surprised us too just how many do fly past. Certainly though, when deciding to lie out of a balmy evening simply to watch the night sky, occasionally one is rewarded with the sudden silver blaze of a 'shooting star' as some fragment of rock burns up on entering the earth's atmosphere.

Being but 230 miles or so north of Egypt, one can imagine why this ancient race worshipped their sun and moon gods and modelled their wonderful pyramid monuments on the constellation of Orion, with the Milky Way as it streams overhead represented by the Nile. It is known that the Egyptians had strong contacts with Cyprus and I often wonder what contribution they may have made to the island's development. They were well ahead of their time with brilliant construction techniques still not understood today. If one scribes a circle, bisects it horizontally, then draws from the ends of the line an equal-sided triangle reaching to the exact top of the circle, you have the precise shape of the great pyramid at Giza. The angle at which the 480 ft high edifice had to be built to achieve this is a very precise 51 degrees and 51 minutes. The stepped stonework we see today was once clad in brilliant white marble limestone sheets ground flat with optical precision, the joints invisible. Gleaming in the sun like the star it is believed to represent, and visible on the desert floor from miles away, the pyramid shape casts a shadow only in the early dawn and at sunset. Not a bad achievement for people who constructed it some 4500 years ago.

Plato tells us that around this time too, an Egyptian scholar noticed how the sun shone directly down a well in Aswan on the day of the summer solstice. The following year at that same time, he travelled north to a well in Cairo and noted how the sun did not shine directly down but was offset slightly. By measuring this angle he calculated that the circumference of the earth was 25,000 miles. All this at a time when man was not supposed to know about *pi* or that the earth was round.

Before leaving the subject of wells, it is worth noting how many owners of property in North Cyprus have wells dug, a sensible thing to do with the island's chronic water problem. How close to sea level the property is, will usually but not necessarily dictate the depth where water will be found. Half-way between the sea and the mountain foothills in the Kyrenia area, the normal depth required before water is reached is between 100 and 150 feet. There are, luckily, several water diviners who can predict the lines along which water is likely to flow. One such gifted genius is a resident Englishman called Rob Vardy. It is fascinating to watch him as, with eyes tightly closed, he slowly walks the terrain seemingly in a deep trance. As water is sensed by the twin rods held out in front of him, one sees them twitch gradually together and cross over. Once the area is pin-pointed, Rob once more walks steadily away, rods still outstretched, until they cross again and give him a reading for the depth at which the water is located and the likely yield. Often, he says, subsequent diggers will inform an owner that his well is finished but how a certain amount of time is necessary before the water gathers and begins to fill it. Sometimes, much to the owner's chagrin, no water arrives at all. Irate customers ring Rob to complain but the answer is always the same; check the depth. Almost always it will be a few metres short of what Rob ordered. 'Well-digging is slow, tiring and dangerous work and the sooner one stops the better', seems to be the local philosophy. Having conducted now some 80 successful surveys, Rob has many tales to tell about his experiences but once he insists that his prescribed depth is reached, the water is always there. And, guess what? From the bottom of a well shaft, the stars are always visible even on the brightest days.

Wells truly are fascinating things and seem to have a folklore all their own. According to local belief, the snow-melt off the Taurus Mountains in Turkey will flow beneath the deep sea channel between the Turkish mainland and Cyprus and fill the wells in our coastal regions with pure, fresh water. The Taurus Mountains, some 50 miles away but seen clearly from Cyprus on cold, dry days, rise to 3000 metres in places and the snow can take several months to thaw sufficiently to push large volumes of water to the Turkish coast and for this strange phenomenon to begin. A family friend, Harry, has a well in his garden in Karşıyaka, some 25 km. to the west of Kyrenia, and he told me once how he wanted to empty it for cleaning and scouring early one September, but found it impossible to do so as it refilled faster than his pump could clear it even after operating for many hours – and it had not rained in Cyprus since April.

CHAPTER IV
A BRIEF HISTORICAL BACKGROUND TO CYPRUS

Before beginning this section, I feel I must put in a personal plea. When I was young and at school, we were taught that Cyprus and the countries comprising the 'Crescent', described in detail below, were referred to as the Near East. Arabia and the sub-continent of India were known as the Middle East, while Thailand, Burma, Singapore, China and Japan comprised the Far East. Today, however, the Middle East seems to start in Libya and extend to the Himalayas. By this measure then it seems to me that the Near East must now originate somewhere around the Old Kent Road. Beef over, we'll return to Cyprus.

It is not my intention to make this a guide book as it must be acknowledged how books written about Cyprus run probably into dozens, many of them dealing with its fascinating history in great detail. My own intention then, is to give some information about its highlights (and lowlights) as a frame-work for my own story. After all, when asked why we live here, the island's long and intriguing history, and the remains still to be glimpsed of its resulting cultures, is very much part of our answer.

41

The island of Cyprus is the third largest in the Mediterranean Sea, behind Sicily and Sardinia, with its length around 140 miles and breadth 60 miles at the widest part. In all, its land area is 3,584 square miles. It is situated 230 miles north of Egypt, 60 miles off Syria, the nearest land to the east, and a mere 40 miles from the Turkish coast that can be seen clearly on fine, dry days. On cold winter days, viewed from the castle at Kantara, one can sometimes see the snows on the distant mountains of Lebanon.

Some of the locals like to describe Cyprus's shape as that of 'a deerskin nailed to a barn door' the four little extremities at each 'corner' suggesting legs and the long, narrow peninsula, known as the Karpaz, forming the tail. Drawing an imaginary line through the island, and using Paphos as the beginning and the tip of the Karpaz as the far end, it runs from south-west to north-east.

According to ancient legend, Cyprus was the birth-place of the celebrated Goddess of Love. She was born out of the sea-foam created by a rock that stands a few hundred metres off shore near Paphos in the south-west of the island. The Romans called the goddess Venus, while the Greeks knew her as Aphrodite, but in other respects she was one and the same. Britain's one-time Prime Minister during Queen Victoria's reign, Benjamin Disraeli, was a great lover of Cyprus and his memorable description of the island is worth quoting; -"Land famous in all ages... the rosy realm of Venus, the romantic Kingdom of the Crusades". The romantic associations continue to this day. I was told recently how Cyprus is the second most popular place in the world, after the

42

West Indies, in which to be married, and the seven Anglican Chaplaincies on the island are kept busy with weddings around the calendar, with most taking place in the summer months. The Paphos Chaplaincy alone has been known to conduct up to six hundred weddings in a single year.

The island of Cyprus must be one of the most fascinating places on earth. At the easternmost end of the Mediterranean, it is surrounded by what the historian Herodotus styled 'the fertile crescent'. Starting at the north coast of the Mediterranean Sea, and moving clockwise using the modern names, we pass through Greece, Turkey, Lebanon, Syria, Israel, Palestine, Jordan and Egypt, recognised as the major states comprising what is also called the 'cradle of civilisation', all venerable in their great past. The area is sometimes also referred to as the Levant, the 'place of the sunrise'. At the time of Christ, the traveller could go from the northern coast of Africa through all these areas, even as far as Britain, without once leaving the Roman Empire. Full citizens of Rome, by the way, were free to do just that. Reminiscent of the star at the middle of the Turkish flag, with its attendant crescent moon, Cyprus sits at the centre of this ancient world.

The travel writer Colin Thubron, in his highly-acclaimed book, *Journey through Cyprus* comments on the countless tracks and paths that have been worn on the island by its inhabitants and visitors over the centuries, observing how the waters around the island would show thousands more tracks going in every possible direction could they somehow be made visible. Taking the occasional boat trip from Kyrenia harbour and moving either west or east, I am confident that those views of North Cyprus we see today, with the ever-present and distinctive backdrop of the Kyrenia Mountain range, would be instantly recognisable by a Roman soldier posted here some 2,000 years ago. (PLATE 4)

If we begin with the earliest known times in Cyprus, there is clear evidence of man's habitation for at least the last 10,000 years, with many prehistoric and Neolithic sites still discernable and most well labelled by the tourist authority. Wandering at random over some land shortly after Meryl and I had bought it in the village of Ozanköy I was thrilled to discover a broken but still recognisable Stone Age axe-head simply lying on the ground where, presumably, it had lain undisturbed for possibly 8,000 years. There are ruins too from the times of the Phoenician and Persian occupations as well as Roman. Well towards the western extremity of the North's territory are the ruins of Vouni, a Persian palace built around the 5th Century BC. Its builders certainly knew how to pick the perfect spot. Sited at the top of a high peak that rises immediately above the sea-shore, it still enjoys breathtaking views over the huge sweep of Morphou Bay. Inland from there to the east is the Roman town of Soli, begun in Hellenistic times, and again mostly in ruins but with some fine early mosaics.

By the first century BC, the Romans had comprehensively colonised Cyprus and wrapped it securely in their Empire. One serious hiccough in this tidy arrangement occurred later when Mark Antony, the Roman Governor of the Eastern Empire, became famously besotted with the Egyptian Queen Cleopatra and presented her with Cyprus as a gift. Such profligacy together with his other misdemeanours did not go down too well with the Roman ruler, Octavian, who despatched a fleet of many warships to help concentrate Antony's mind and to restore order, resulting in the sea battle of Actium which Antony's side lost. As is well known, the defeat caused Antony and then Cleopatra to commit suicide. Depressing though these events were, they at least gave Shakespeare an opportunity to write another of his gripping tragedies.

Although today the Karpaz peninsula looks relatively untouched by civilisation, several Roman cities once existed along its north coast and the occasional drowned harbour can still be discerned through the crystal waters. In many areas along the Karpaz, the ground is littered with shards of Roman pottery, glass, broken pillars, large fragments of dressed stone and other artefacts. The village of Sipahi, towards the northern end of the peninsula, has on its outskirts a ruined 6th Century Byzantine church but with its lovely mosaic floor still in fine condition, despite being exposed to the elements, and keeping the surrounding vegetation at bay. Only the wind drifting through the trees and rustling the long grasses, with the soft sound of tinkling sheep bells sometimes added, disturb the silence of this serene spot. Among the many mosaic designs, there is one illustrating what must be the very first pair of 'flip-flops'. Who would have thought they were such an early invention? However, in conjunction with the shell motif the sandals are, in fact, symbols of the pilgrim.

When the Roman Empire began disintegrating in the 4th Century AD, Cyprus, like so many other parts, was left defenceless and almost immediately became vulnerable to raids by neighbouring races eager to plunder her riches of copper ore and timber as well as to harness the inhabitants into virtual slavery. Incidentally, some historians say that copper (Latin, *cyprium aes*, Cyprus metal) was named after Cyprus and others that Cyprus was named after copper (Late Latin, *cuprum*).

For all its difficult past, Cyprus became in the 4th Century AD the very first country to have a Christian ruler. It had been visited by St Paul and his fellow disciples Mark and Barnabas, the latter a Cypriot by birth. St Andrew too came to Cyprus by sea with his shipmates desperate for water after their voyage. Like Moses before him in the Sinai desert, Andrew struck a rock above the shore at the far northern extremity of the Karpaz peninsula, whereupon water gushed forth. To celebrate this miracle, a monastery was later built on the site and pilgrimages began, seeking the saint's help. Even today, St Andrew is credited with many miraculous cures, and the small monastery is still served by the local Greek community living in the nearby village of Dip Karpaz. The building is filled to bursting with crystal chandeliers, votive candles and silvered-over icons of the saints, with St Andrew's spring still gurgling beneath the altar. It is of tremendous religious importance to the Greek Cypriots, who come in their thousands

46

to make pilgrimage to the monastery on St Andrew's Day, the 30th November. Recently, as part of a UN-funded scheme, the accommodation for pilgrims, built originally around 100 years ago when it probably took several days by camel or donkey to travel from the island's extremities, has been carefully restored and the monastery itself, although not so very old, is shortly to receive similar attention, long overdue.

The disciple Barnabas also added substantially to the legends of Cyprus. When he died around 50 AD, he was buried near to the old Roman capital of Salamis in the east of the island, his exact burial place unknown. However, in 478 his tomb was discovered in a catacomb close to the coast, with the saint's remains clasping what was claimed to be the copy he'd made of St Matthew's Gospel. This priceless treasure was duly presented to the Emperor Zeno in Constantinople, nowadays Istanbul, and at that time the religious control centre for Cyprus, but so pleased was his Imperial Majesty with the gift that he conferred in return on all Archbishops of Cyprus in perpetuity the right to wear a purple cope and to carry a sceptre instead of the pastoral staff. Also granted was the right to sign documents in red ink, considered still a great privilege. Most important of all to the Church in Cyprus, however, was the granting of self-governing status.

This momentous event was commemorated later by the construction of St Barnabas' Monastery just a few steps away from the Saint's burial chamber carved deep in the rock and reached by a flight of steps down into the catacomb. Today the abbey church is an icon museum operated by the Tourist Authority of the Turkish Cypriot government, with the former cells of the monks turned into another museum containing many relics found in the excavated graves that seem to turn up on an amazingly regular basis as roads and buildings are developed in the Karpaz district. This museum is well worth a visit and contains some beautiful pottery such as bowls, vases, jugs and amphorae for wine and oil, most of it surprisingly elegant in design. The decorations too, usually ivory-coloured on the clay-coloured pottery, or black against the creamy ceramic ware, look deceptively modern. Most charming of all for me are the exquisite children's toys, also modelled brilliantly from clay and presumably set originally in a child's grave to console it in its afterlife. There are chariots pulled by horses, with wheels obviously capable of turning on their axles and what could easily pass for doll's house furniture too among many other lovely and touching treasures carefully moulded for lost children. (PLATE 5) In the monastery's courtyard early one spring we visited the pleasant café there and watched enthralled as noisy swallows, busy feeding their young in the several nests high above the customers' heads, swooped fearlessly in and out of the room.

At the beginning of the second millennium, Europe slowly began to stir and came under strong obligation from the Church to remove the Infidel from the Holy Land, thus launching what we know today as the Crusades. With most of the European countries having embraced Christianity by this time, England was no exception to this objective and wholeheartedly joined in the sacred journeys to the East.

England's greatest hero of this period was King Richard the Lionheart. Sailing out from England on his journey in 1191, the fleet was accompanied by a ship bearing Richard's fiancée, Berengaria. St Paul was by no means the first to be shipwrecked in the Mediterranean and Richard's fleet was badly mauled in a severe storm off Rhodes and the ships were scattered. A further storm near to Cyprus again separated the fleet and wrecked two of Richard's ships off the port of Limassol in the south. Happily, the vessel in that group bearing Berengaria reached a safe anchorage off the port, but then became the target of Isaac, the self-styled Emperor of Cyprus, who saw these tragedies as an opportunity to plunder the two wrecks and to hold Berengaria hostage for ransom. In fact, the second part of his plan backfired badly as her ship managed to put out to sea again and rejoin Richard's fleet, thus escaping Isaac's greedy clutches. Even so, Richard was not the kind of king to tolerate such effrontery, so he promptly landed to set about teaching the Emperor a lesson.

The outcome of the resulting skirmishes found Isaac imprisoned and Richard, as conqueror, in sole charge of the island. Curiously, Isaac begged Richard not to bind him in iron, so Richard obligingly had silver chains made for his ankles and gold for his wrists. It is not recorded whether the now ex-Emperor was pleased with this concession. In the meantime, so relieved and delighted was Richard to recover his bride-to-be safely that they were married immediately at Limassol in a small chapel there. Thus, Richard was the first and only monarch of England to be married on foreign soil and, with Berengaria anointed

Queen of England, that too was the first and only such occasion of its type to be held outside England.

Before we leave the south it is worth noting how Lazarus, whom Christ raised from the dead, is claimed to have voyaged across to Cyprus from Palestine and to have become the first Bishop of Kition, the old Roman name for modern-day Larnaca.

Moving on from Cyprus to the Holy Land, Richard found the fighting hard going, his chief adversary being the legendary Saladin, commander of the Muslim forces, benefiting from fighting on his own territory and just as committed as the Crusaders to a Holy War. Despite the ferocity of the fighting and the immense cruelty to both horses and men in the battles, the age of chivalry was just beginning to flower. According to a well-established tradition, Richard's horse was killed under him by an arrow in the midst of battle, an incident observed by Saladin who promptly sent over a replacement charger for the king.

Richard's treasury was sorely strapped for the cash needed to continue the Crusade and to pay his men, so he sold Cyprus to the Knights Templar for the sum of 100,000 Bezants. If the currency sounds rather unusual, it is worth explaining how the word Bezant derived from 'Byzantius', the adjective of Byzantium (now Istanbul), where the gold and silver coins were minted.

However, the Knights Templar soon found the burden of Cyprus too great and begged Richard to take it back again. Although the Knights had paid only 40,000 Bezants deposit, as so often happens with these deals, Richard had long since spent the money. The Knights lost out considerably but their prudence kept financial damage to the minimum. Among Richard's chums at the battle front was one Guy de Lusignan, a distinguished nobleman from France. By marriage, Guy was entitled to the 'Kingdom of Jerusalem', but had recently been widowed, causing the title to pass him by, and leaving him unemployed. Richard offered him Cyprus by way of compensation, thus creating a family dynasty that was to last for nearly 300 years. Early on in Guy's reign and in order to fortify the island against further attacks from Arab raiding parties, existing castles on the Kyrenia mountain range and at the ports were extended and strengthened.

The Crusaders were finally expelled from the Holy Land after the fall of Acre in 1291. The Christian remnant that survived the struggle was obliged to withdraw to Famagusta and by the 14th Century the town was reckoned to have become the wealthiest city in the Western world. The old trade routes from the East across India, Iraq, Iran and Saudi Arabia bringing silks from China, spices from India and precious stones from the mines of Maharajahs terminated in Palestine, but that and all surrounding lands were firmly back now in the grip of the Infidel. Cyprus, with its city of Famagusta, was the nearest point of civilisation to the Holy Land and a wide expanse of the Mediterranean Sea formed a comforting barrier between the Barbarians and the Christians' new outpost. Even the lands to the north and south of Palestine were territories occupied by the arch-enemy so there was no safe alternative to the new retreat. Despite the difficulties of traversing the trade routes, the wealth from the east that was destined for western markets seemed to be concentrated securely in Famagusta by tacit agreement with all the parties concerned.

At Famagusta, I always feel as though going through a time-warp when crossing the moat bridge, entering under the portcullis, through the tunnel beneath the massive bastions and into the old walled town. The Greek name 'Ammochostos' means 'lost in the sands' and that is exactly what happened to Salamis, the Roman capital just a mile or two to the north, as a result of a combination of earthquakes and raids, and the subsequent plundering of its stones over the intervening centuries. 'Famagusta' on the other hand, is said to be a Lusignan corruption of the old Greek name, Ammochostos (hidden in the sun). Today, many houses, gardens and other buildings throughout Cyprus show clear evidence of Roman masonry; pillars, columns and dressed stonework as well as more obvious artefacts such as the beautifully carved marble sarcophagus at Bellapais Abbey that the medieval monks took away and used as a lavatorium, that is to say, a washing place. Around the ancient harbour in Kyrenia, bollards for securing boats are truncated marble columns scavenged from Roman ruins, while a short causeway out to the old chain tower is made partly from small baluster shafts laid horizontally, that originally held up altars built for the Roman gods. Despite this vandalism, archaeologists allege that eighty-five per cent of Salamis is still covered by sand and await future excavation. What wonderful treasures must lie there, waiting to be discovered.

The fabled walls still surrounding Famagusta old town are the work of the Venetians in the 15th and 16th centuries when they virtually re-built the principal cities of the times. The key port of Famagusta was considered to be especially vulnerable to attacks from the sea by Barbarians, correctly as it turned out, so massive walls were constructed some 20 and 30 feet thick in places, further protected all around the outside by a wide and deep moat. Set into the corner nearest the port is a separate castle still called 'Othello's Tower'. The Bard referred to 'A Sea Port in Cyprus' when writing his 'tragedy of a handkerchief' as the play is sometimes referred to. Tradition and research indicate that the 'port' is indeed Famagusta as there is also well-documented evidence that an appointee from Venice called Cristophoro Moro had charge of Famagusta around 1508. Significantly, Moro lost his wife on the way back to Venice after his term of office expired although the circumstances of her death are unknown. With a mind as sharply honed as Shakespeare's, it would have been a simple matter to shift the Venetian's name to Moor, and to turn him into a black man as a means of cranking up the tension a notch or two. Shakespeare wrote the tragedy in 1604 when the heroic defence of Famagusta against the Turks in 1571 was still green in the public memory, and the town itself, when under Venetian control, used to rival both her parent city and Genoa in terms of wealth and prestige. Many are the stories told of the profligate life-style of the wealthy merchants of medieval Famagusta. Kings were regularly entertained to fabulous banquets cooked over fires of priceless sandalwood with caskets of valuable jewellery given to each diner at the feast. On one such occasion, two wealthy merchant brothers offered drinks containing pearls and other jewels of immense value ground up with mortar and pestle – opulence gone mad – merely to impress their guests.

Once inside the town, the visitor sees how it is still dreaming of the grandeur of its former medieval days with its many churches and the magnificent cathedral dominating all. In its heyday, Famagusta allegedly possessed no fewer than 365 churches, many of them small admittedly, and some built as an act of piety or sometimes to atone for sins. According to legend one such attractive small church was built at the expense of 'a lady of the night' in the hope that it might militate in her favour when she reached the heavenly gate. Another was erected in fulfilment of a promise to God should the merchant's ship, heavily laden with valuables, reach port safely. Most of the churches have vanished and those remaining are now in ruins or what the poet John Betjeman called in another place 'pleasing decay', while the cathedral was converted to a mosque by the triumphant Turks following their conquest. Others have compared the ruined churches with 'hummocks of sheep peacefully grazing the city's pasture', both descriptions pleasing to me. In fact, thanks to the armoured Venetian fortifications, the defenders of Famagusta managed to hold out against the Turkish siege for many months, locked securely within the impregnable fortress. Over that period, however, Turkish ships standing off-shore and besieging troops on shore steadily shelled and catapulted the city with heavy, stone cannon balls. Not surprising then, how so much of the town and its buildings were damaged, with little escaping the wrath of the frustrated invaders and so some of Famagusta's old town remains the same still. Sadly, however, it has to be recorded here that the full destruction seen today was not caused entirely by the Turkish bombardment. During the 1960s, Greek Cypriots possessed several artillery pieces emplaced in their nearby suburb of Famagusta, known as Varosha, from which they routinely shelled at random the traditionally-Turkish old town.

On entering through the land gate, from the big 'monument' roundabout, it is worthwhile parking just inside and climbing the cannon ramp alongside the arch to the top of the walls. From there, one gets a perfect view of the town's layout, the former cathedral with its minaret added once the invaders turned it into a mosque, now dominating the centre with the sea beyond. (PLATE 6) One can imagine the incoming Turkish bombardment and judge just how effective it must have been in razing many of the ancient buildings. To the west, from this vantage point, can also be seen the oblong section of the fortress protruding outwards from the wall's corners and known as the Martinengo bastion, named after the Venetian military architect who designed it and supervised its building. Capable of bringing down withering cannon fire along the walls and the moat from its gun-ports aligned in two directions, it was wisely left alone by the invading Turks.

The cathedral of St Nicholas was built in the 14th Century by the Lusignans as a church where each sovereign's second coronation could be conducted, as Famagusta was geographically slightly nearer to Jerusalem than the cathedral in Nicosia. Here, with full pomp and ceremony, they were formally crowned Kings of Jerusalem, which they saw as their right, having already been crowned Kings of Cyprus in St Sophia, Nicosia. The pointed tops of the beautifully decorated triple arches framing the three doors in the west façade provide elegant framework for a long balcony behind, from which the new, doubly-crowned monarch would show himself to his subjects thronged in the square below.

The Venetians turned their attentions too to Nicosia, the traditional capital of the island from the 10th Century onwards. That also was fortified at enormous cost to the original Lusignan layout of the city. Houses, churches, abbeys and even palaces were demolished in order to bring everything within an almost impregnable circular fortress some four miles in circumference and featuring eleven protruding bastions, curiously shaped like the 'spade' seen on playing cards. The walls were pierced by only three narrow gates – those of Paphos, Kyrenia, and Famagusta – allowing strictly limited access to and from the other main towns of the small island. By ensuring that not one stone stood upon another outside Nicosia's new walls, the Venetian cannon mounted in ravelins around the wall's top were permitted a clear field of fire in any direction in the event of attack.

The fine Gothic cathedral of St Sophia, begun by visiting French builders in the early 13th Century, and also used since the Turkish conquest of 1571 as a mosque, shows poignant evidence, together with other ancient buildings surrounding it, of the lost beauty of Lusignan architecture outside the reinforced capital. Again, the cathedral also contains material brought from the ruins of Salamis and elsewhere. The heavy, turned and tapered pillars that support the apse and choir at the east end are almost 'hall-marked' Roman, even beneath their present-day coats of paint. (PLATE 7)

In the 1950s, an English gentleman named Rupert Gunnis held the post of Keeper of the Antiquities in Cyprus and I have sometimes wondered whether he might have taken his job title too literally. Fascinated by the island's deep history, he carried out many excavations beyond the Venetian walls of Nicosia and recovered great numbers of artefacts, chiefly architectural. As well as helping stock the museums, his enthusiasm and success resulted in the magnificent house he subsequently built in what is now north Nicosia (or Lefkoşa, on the Turkish side) that incorporates many of his finds. Earlier, in 1936, Mr Gunnis wrote a fascinating book called *Historic Cyprus*, sub-titled *A Guide to its Towns and Villages, Monasteries and Castles* and, as one would expect from him, the scholarship is thorough and the accounts well-researched. By way of introduction to each area of the island, he gives an erudite summary of the history of the towns and villages in whose areas the buildings are to be found. His house and its beautiful gardens are liberally furnished with recovered Lusignan stone arches and ancient masonry from other eras, and it is now owned and used by the British Government as its High Commission Office in the north, and is very well looked after, as it should be.

It is interesting to note how, before the Turkish Intervention of 1974, this building housed the British High Commission for the entire island but became marooned in the Turkish sector after the events of that time. Another suitable house was purchased for the Commission afterwards just across the Green Line and, ironically, backing on to the Gunnis house. Shortly after the new place was set up, there was talk of linking the two residences by means of a bridge across the deep ravine that divides them but the plan came to grief on the usual rocky island politics.

Incidentally, the so-called 'Green Line' that divides the city was originally marked out with a green crayon by a British soldier, General Young, on a map in the house's dining room. The rest of the island's dividing boundary is referred to as the 'buffer zone' patrolled by the UN, and this completes the separation of Greek and Turkish territories. Today, the Gunnis house is still used to host meetings and functions the High Commissioner wishes to preside over or hold in the North. There is an elegant dining room, a reception room, a salon and conference room and some offices. A British caretaker lives in a specially prepared flat upstairs and, as well as looking after the building and its operations, enjoys the peace and tranquillity of this charming setting in Lefkoşa. In a corner of the front garden, to the side of the grand entrance, is a recently built consular office, empowered to issue passports for the resident British in the North and to process visas for Turkish Cypriots.

After the sea change in the fortunes of Cyprus brought about by the actions of King Richard and his followers, the Lusignans and their successors, including the Venetians and the Genoese, were known as the 'Latins' and their influence and control in the name of the Roman Catholic Church was bitterly resented by the populace, mainly followers of the Orthodox Church of Cyprus or Islam in the case of the Turkish citizens. The Lusignans seemed to carry in their genes the seeds for their own destruction, as the rivalries between offspring of the kings and queens passed through the generations bickering and quarrelling as they progressed. Again, the many history books about Cyprus cover this period in great detail, but the results of the internecine strife led to the island's eventual take-over by the Venetians in 1489, thus reducing the Kingdom of Cyprus to a mere province of Venice.

The overall situation hardly changed for the Cypriots until the attack by Turkey nearly a hundred years later in 1571 when the island fell by force of arms and the hated Latins were finally defeated and banished. The Ottoman reign lasted almost three hundred years, but proved a tolerant conquest with the Orthodox Cypriots permitted to follow their religion unhindered.

Things changed again when, through political bargaining, Britain accepted responsibility for Cyprus in 1878, and finally brought her into the Empire as part of the settlement of territories following World War 1. At that time, Cyprus was of immense strategic importance to the British as it was an excellent base from which to defend the Suez Canal. Again, in the Confessional it has to be related how the British, early on in their rule, shipped to Egypt dressed stone and other building materials plundered from the debris in Famagusta old town, in order to help build Port Said at the head of the Canal.

Shortly after the British took over responsibility for Cyprus in 1878, journalists and artists from Britain began to visit the island to record information about the Empire's new responsibility. Many of their reports were published in the London Illustrated News over a period of time and today reprints of the articles and accompanying drawings are available and very interesting they are too, when one compares the island then and now. Some of those Victorian engravings show camel trains crossing the Mesaoria plain, at that time the only way of transporting heavy goods and materials from the main port of Famagusta to Nicosia, some fifty miles away. Old khans, or hostelries in Nicosia where the animals with their precious cargoes and the owners could rest overnight in security, date from the 16th Century and have been carefully restored in recent years. The old khans in the Near East had high and wide double wooden doors at their entrances to permit the camels to enter with their loads. However, once all were inside for the night the great doors were secured and a small inner door, built into one of the larger ones, would allow a man to slip through. This door is traditionally known as the 'eye of the needle' and it is thought that Jesus was making reference to it when He declared it would be easier for a camel to pass through the eye of a needle than for a rich man to enter the Kingdom of Heaven.

Sadly, these graceful animals with their slow, plodding gait and haughty expressions have long since disappeared from the Cyprus landscape, but still seen occasionally in the villages are mules and donkeys, also with centuries of service on the island, and even today used as beasts of burden by a few of the poorer people. At the very tip of the Karpaz peninsula, there are some herds of wild donkeys protected now by the State with many of them corralled for their safety in specially enclosed areas. I have read that they are the only wild donkeys left in the Mediterranean.

The later years

Over the past few years, a greater awareness of the environment has begun developing slowly in North Cyprus. It has been reported in the local press how EC directives are being studied and to some extent applied here with the result that the island's rich diversity of plants and wild life is being recognised and, at last, valued as part of the attractions that bring 'specialist' tourists to visit. As the more informed articles point out, as well as being good for tourism, the directives once implemented are good for the people who live here too. The inestimable value of the farmlands on the Mesaoria Plain has already been acknowledged elsewhere in this book but it is now being described as a treasure-trove of wild plants and animals, by visiting wild-life experts. This special area is still providing a perfect habitat for species of birds that are endangered in other parts of Europe, such as blue rollers, melodic calandra larks, corn buntings, black-headed buntings, and linnets all of which are present here in good numbers.

Among the ex-pat community, north and south, it is widely hoped that EU directives will put an end to the senseless slaughter of tens of thousands of wild birds when the shooting seasons of spring and autumn are finally outlawed. It was reported a few years ago how half a million birds were killed in the south on a single day, when the spring season opened. Whilst one might learn to tolerate an autumn season, it seems madness to allow another in the spring when the poor creatures are breeding.

On the north coast, there are several sandy beaches where Loggerhead and Green turtles come ashore to breed, both also highly endangered species. Over the last few years students from British universities have been coming across during the summer months to help identify nesting sites and to protect them from interference, either animal or human. They set up temporary residence on the beaches to ensure they can operate surveillance around the clock and to help the new hatchlings make their way safely to the sea. Here, credit for beginning this project and doing a great deal of the work themselves initially, as well as drawing international attention to the conservation of these delightful creatures, must go to a charming British couple formerly resident in North Cyprus, Ian and Celia Bell.

The Troodos Mountains in the south are home to a unique wild sheep, the Cyprus mouflon, although after decades of hunting, it is feared to have become extinct as none has been seen for some time. More plentiful creatures though still exist elsewhere such as the Cyprus grass snake and endemic birds like the attractive black and white Cyprus wheatear, the Cyprus warbler, the Cyprus coal tit and the prettily-named Cyprus short-toed tree-creeper, the latter, like the mouflon, found chiefly in the pine forests of the Troodos.

The domestic donkeys, such patient creatures with their quiet way of standing and sad expressions, seem to be contemplating the fate that cast them in their humble role. (PLATE 8) It appears to me that the smaller the animal and the thinner its legs, the larger the man slouched over its back will prove to be. However, today's donkeys are well looked after and valued by their owners and are much stronger than their small frames suggest. But it always cheers me to recall those wonderful lines from GK Chesterton's poem, entitled 'The Donkey':

'When fishes flew and forests walked

And fig grew upon thorn

Some moment when the moon was blood

Then, surely, I was born'.

It ends:

'Fools! For I also had my hour

There was a shout about my ears

And palms before my feet'.

If one looks carefully, most donkeys still carry the Cross of Jesus in the shaded patterns of the hair across their backs.

As if to speed up the replacement of the camels, the British constructed a narrow-gauge railway to carry freight from Famagusta to Nicosia and then on to Morphou in the north-west of the island, a town now called Güzelyurt, translated as 'beautiful place' from the Turkish. At the time of the construction of this section of the line copper ore was still being mined in the Morphou area and the railway was used primarily to ship the material to Famagusta's port. And today, Güzelyurt is indeed still beautiful; where the citrus orchards are located, producing oranges, lemons, grapefruit, bergamot - and also avocados. At Güzelyurt there is an original locomotive set up at the side of the road as a memorial to this railway, and another sits in Famagusta outside the former main railway office next to the hospital.

Although the British Empire remains a favourite target for the cynics who prefer to believe we did nothing to help the local populace wherever we went, but merely exploited the land and its people, in Cyprus Britain introduced many benefits that are still appreciated today.

Proper roads were constructed where there were only tracks before; hospitals were built and supplied with skilled staff; schools created with excellent teaching, and other educational facilities provided. The islanders still drive on the left and, although painted yellow as the preferred colour outside the UK, cast-iron pillar boxes remain scattered over the towns and villages, their original Royal Ciphers still in place and surprisingly, sometimes picked out in black. (PLATE 9) The British system of justice was brought in and administered by experienced colonial officials and staff. Even today, many of the older Turkish Cypriots mourn the passing of the former British administration, seen still as honest, fair and impartial. It also protected the Turkish minority as, in the early Fifties when the 'Troubles' began, the Turkish Cypriots were outnumbered four to one in favour of the Greek Cypriots.

As with the long and fascinating history of Cyprus, I have to say that many books, pamphlets and newspaper articles, not to mention documentaries on film and television, have been produced about the circumstances leading up to the present-day division of the island. Again, it is not my intention to embark on a full analysis of the events of the past 50 years, but only to set out a brief synopsis as might fit this book.

In the 1930s unrest began to be fomented against the British occupation of the island, chiefly by the Greek Cypriot element, with a state of emergency being declared in 1931. The end of World War II saw the beginning of stirrings in the world for a chance at freedom and independence as the dust settled again in Europe, and the Nazi tyranny was finally broken. The Indian subcontinent too was anxious to throw off the British yoke and yearned for true independence after almost three hundred years of British rule. The Greek Cypriots looked around them and saw significant progress being made in other countries with what they saw as a problem similar to their own.

America, believing that the war had weakened Britain morally and financially, saw an opportunity to take over gradually the role of 'World Policeman' by usurping Britain's power and influence, thus directing the benefits of Empire to their own advantage. In short, then, the Fifties were a time of change in the World Order and no one realised this more than the Greek Cypriots.

At first there were protests and similar attempts at civil disobedience. These developed into strikes and accompanying violence. Eventually, a full revolt gradually began, with the setting up of EOKA, which was a Greek Cypriot organisation dedicated to guerrilla warfare against the British. Arms were smuggled into the island from Greece with the connivance and cooperation of the Greek government, and soon serious insurrection was common and well organised. The British used their time-honoured methods of dealing with the growing problem by using the island's British police force as well as the armed forces in an attempt to root out the culprits and bring them to justice. EOKA's tactics were unsubtle and brutally effective. It operated on a simple premise – either you are for us or against

66

us. Anyone in the latter category, and that included many Greek Cypriots, was considered a fair target and often treated in the same way as the British.

There was little discrimination, either, about who got killed. British servicemen were shot in the back while patrolling the streets of the capital or of other large towns. Occasionally, it was British housewives, gunned down while going about their daily business. The well-known President of Cyprus in these times was Archbishop Makarios, a haughty, proud cleric who seemed ambivalent in his attitude towards the British and to the Greek Cypriots whom he represented. Even so, he did little to stop the bloodshed and is suspected of encouraging privately much of the violence. He was also very much in the pockets of the mainland Greeks at that time and the objective of EOKA became 'Enosis' or union with Greece itself. It is a favourite myth of the Greek Cypriots that the island belonged at one time in its distant past to Greece, but it never did; the Ottoman Empire, yes, but Greece, no. Ironically, Cyprus was offered to Greece by the British Government during the First World War if they would agree to support the Allies against Germany, but the proposal was turned down.

Eventually, in 1960, the British conceded the independence of Cyprus and left the island, but, under the Treaty of Guarantee, Turkey, Greece and Britain were appointed as 'Guarantor Powers' to ensure that the newly drawn up Constitution was adhered to and that Cyprus would be properly and fairly governed. Among other things, the new arrangement provided for the minority Turkish Cypriot population to be given fair representation in government, the civil service and other government-controlled areas such as schools, hospitals, customs and police.

In return for granting independence, Britain retained two areas, each comprising several square miles of land on the south coast of the island in order to continue to operate its army and air-force bases. These were considered essential by NATO, which included the US, of course, as Cyprus was by that time the last outpost of British territory in the Near East. Again, a quick look at a map of the eastern basin of the Mediterranean and the surrounding lands will show how there are no other places where such bases could be accommodated securely and also why it was and still is, despite the arrival of spy satellites, essential to know what's going on in the area. The 'listening' equipment installed at these bases is, and always has been, the most sophisticated available in the world, much of it still top-secret.

Sadly, and inevitably perhaps, the new Cyprus did not adhere to its early promises. Within a very short time, the Greek Cypriots began to isolate their Turkish brethren: they were gradually and clandestinely removed from positions of authority in all areas of administration of the island and their persecution began in earnest. To their lasting shame, the Greeks embarked on a campaign they code-named 'The Akritas Plan', which was simply the eradication of all Turkish Cypriots on the island, or what we now call 'genocide'.

Appeals for help by the beleaguered Turkish minority fell on deaf ears, with Greece not surprisingly looking the other way and Britain shamefully more concerned over its Sovereign Bases which required the goodwill and wholehearted cooperation of the Greek Cypriots in order to operate at all. Turkey was warned to keep off Cyprus by other key powers, with the US leading the urge for caution. Over the years, the plight of the Turkish Cypriots became more and more desperate, with women and children routinely massacred as well as their men folk. In all, no fewer than 103 Turkish villages were evacuated, leaving thousands homeless. Those still alive after these atrocities were forced to take refuge in safe villages that became enclaves for wretched Turkish Cypriots fighting for their very survival. Aware of the dire circumstances, many young Turkish Cypriot men, some of them students in European countries including Britain, travelled overland via Turkey to reach the island and participate in fighting off the Greek onslaught.

The small area of Erenköy, a thumbnail of Turkish Cypriot territory embedded into a part of the north coast held by the Greek side is one such place where in 1964 an heroic stand was made by the Turkish Cypriots, supported by air strikes flown from bases on the Turkish mainland. A force of a few hundred managed to hold off concerted and sustained attacks, unprecedented in their ferocity. On this shameful occasion, well-armed and equipped troops from Greece also took part. Had it not been for the careful diplomacy of the UN staff, forbidden by law to intervene, but trying to hold off the full thrust of these merciless attacks, the Turkish defenders would almost certainly have been massacred to the last man. As it is, several young men are buried in a small cemetery at Erenköy, more-or-less where they fell at that fateful time. Because the area was under constant bombardment, it was necessary to carry out the burials during the night.

During my first year in North Cyprus I tried without success to join the annual trek that takes place always on August 8th to Erenköy; so intriguingly marked out on the official tourist maps but closed to visitors at all other times of the year. Only the Turkish military are permitted to stay there for security purposes.

The following year though I was lucky and together with three English friends managed to book passage on the specially chartered ship that bore us and around 850 Turkish Cypriots along the coast. A last-minute dispute by the Greek authorities, who steadfastly refused to allow the visitors to pass through Greek-held land, meant that urgent plans had to be made to go by sea, and it was a tribute to Kutlay Keco (Jimmy, of the Grapevine) who also fought at Erenköy and survived, that such elaborate and complicated arrangements could be completed in such a miraculously short time. Boarding at 3 a.m. and sailing by deep starlight at 4 a.m meant an almost impossibly early start for babes in arms, small children and elderly people alike.

Far from there being a resentful mood among our fellow passengers, they were quietly happy under any conditions to be going back to their beloved former homes and to pay annual homage to the fallen. Each family had come prepared for the long day with baskets containing food and bottled water. Fergün Feris of North Cyprus, who

70

had supplied the vessel, had also provided a cafeteria to supplement refreshments with hot coffee, tea and other drinks as well as sandwiches. Many pilgrims, for I feel I must describe them as such, carried bouquets, wreaths or large bunches of flowers to dress the hallowed graves.

Despite chronic overcrowding, the voyage was enjoyed with good-humour, quiet tolerance and goodwill all round in the shared discomfort. The greatest feeling of satisfaction was reached when the ship, entering coastal waters off Erenköy, was "buzzed" by a Greek patrol boat, its fore-deck dominated by heavy machine gun. A spontaneous but united roar went up from the whole ship followed by sardonic hand clapping. The patrol boat sheered away, clearly deflated by its fearless reception. That incident in itself was a memorable moment and seemed to set the atmosphere of determination and defiance for which Erenköy is fabled.

As the large ferry was unable to get close to land, the full ship's complement of passengers was painstakingly ferried ashore by TRNC coastguard vessels and an army landing craft capable of holding around 100 passengers. Even so, it was a lengthy and hazardous business but again, borne stoically by young and old together. Ironically, the only "casualty" of this part of the operation was a member of our own party who, misjudging the sea swell while transferring, fell awkwardly into the boat and sustained a painful injury to his back. It was this accident, however, that seemed to bring out that wonderful spirit of the Turkish Cypriot people. Typically, a quite elderly man jumped down and ran ahead when we reached a specially designated landing stage to alert the UN medical staff that our friend urgently needed help. It seemed that from then on we were treated more like VIPs than interlopers at a family scene, with our colleague then being taken into the highly skilled care of the doctors of the resident Turkish Army.

The service at the Erenköy cemetery was a moving affair. The graves themselves are lovingly tended and maintained, and lie under the cool shade of evergreens and flowering shrubs. Thirteen young student defenders rest there, each tomb bearing a contemporary photograph of its occupant, smiling out from his sixties' clothing and Beatle haircut. Each grave was quickly decked out in the floral decorations brought so carefully by loving relations. Family groups surrounded each one, the elders quiet and pensive, many with their lips moving silently in prayer, the young toddlers balancing with outstretched arms as they gambolled innocently along the coping stones. It was a deeply affecting spectacle.

Official speeches were brief but eloquent, plainly free from demagogy and rancour. Although to our shame, none of us understood Turkish, it was sufficient to absorb the deep emotion that poured out not only from the speakers themselves but also from everyone that took part. The wonderful cadences of President Denktaş, who retired from office in April 2005 after some fifty years of service to his country, were more redolent of reconciliation than revenge. I watched, greatly moved, as he carefully placed a single flower on each particular grave with as much tenderness and reverence as though it were his own family interred there. I suppose on reflection that is exactly as he did see it, as Mr Denktaş was himself at Erenköy for a short time and helped bury some of the youngsters so each of the young men was known personally to him.

The ceremonies over, we were able to check up on the progress of our injured chum who, by this time had been thoroughly examined independently by no fewer than three army doctors. Happily, they were united in their view that he had suffered no serious injury, no fractures anywhere, just very severe bruising. Complete rest until we had to move out was the order, so the remaining three of us wandered up the coast for a mile or so to see one of the shattered villages, left as it was 36 years ago as a monument to the sacrifice of the young men. The most distressing sight in our view was the truncated minaret of the village mosque, the top having been carried away during an artillery bombardment.

In many of the ruined houses small groups were gathered, some standing and remembering, some weeping openly at the still-felt pain of their irretrievable loss. Others sat on bare earth where their former residence had once stood, serene faces recalling perhaps what had once been a happy part of their lives and their youth. For myself, I no longer felt part of things as I had at the orations and military pomp in the graveyard. This seemed more like an intrusion into their privacy and I had no desire to watch the families trying still to come to terms with their continuing suffering. And yet, here I was indeed joining in and empathising with all these emotions. Though I had been apprehensive at the outset of the journey, and uncertain of what to expect, all suddenly became clear and filled me with a sense of solidarity that I was sharing all this with so many Turkish Cypriot families.

At around 1 o'clock, it was time to begin the laborious task of embarking the passengers for the return voyage. We were still much concerned for our injured colleague but, thanks to the intervention of Kutlay Keco who has a tremendous rapport with the army, arrangements were made for us to return across the bay in the army's landing craft with another group, mainly service personnel, to the port of Gemikonağı, just over the border into TRNC territory. There, we would have the choice of an ambulance to carry our chum to the local hospital or an army staff bus to go through to Girne if he felt fit enough for the journey. While all this was being arranged, our small party was kept well supplied by the army with both hot and cold drinks. In the event, he took the latter option and we arrived back in Girne in the late afternoon.

To this day, the still-ruined villages of the area are preserved in that state as a symbolic reminder of the appalling hardships the Turkish Cypriots had to suffer and survive in order to achieve the statehood they enjoy today.

Despite a lull in events and countless attempts to resolve the problems between the Turkish and Greek Cypriots, nothing really changed, and in the early seventies the situation again deteriorated. Meanwhile, matters were being fomented in Greece itself as the so-called 'Colonels' Junta' in Athens instigated a coup in Cyprus to usurp Makarios, take over government and clinch the Enosis issue once and for all. As 1974 wore on, the Turkish government became more and more frustrated with the other major powers that seemed uninterested in interfering in these latest developments or in coming to the aid of the Turkish Cypriots in their extreme circumstances. All Turkey's many appeals to Britain, Greece and the US fell on deaf ears.

Finally, with the clandestine connivance, it is believed, of the Americans, Turkey began an all-out armed assault on Cyprus on July 20th with troops, artillery and tanks landing on the coast to the west of Kyrenia and paratroopers dropping into the foothills, all supported by fighter aircraft and bombers. After the remarkably short time of three days the battle was won and the clearing up process started that resulted in the arrangement we see today.

The Turkish Cypriots claim, with full justification, how peace on the island has been maintained ever since the intervention by Turkey in July 1974, not only for themselves but also for the Greek Cypriots, many of whom were killed if they dared speak out against the butchery of their fellow Cypriots or disagree with the feared EOKA terrorists.

CHAPTER V
RENTING A HOUSE

The flat in Croydon sold, it was time to set off for North Cyprus together with possessions for our immediate needs once we had arrived, the main effects following by sea. At Heathrow, there was some excitement when our 11 bags were checked in and weighed. Fortunately, a pleasant and helpful young lady was on duty at the check-in counter that day and our luggage was not too much overweight. Meryl told me afterwards how my foot appeared to have become trapped on our side on the scales, preventing them from descending too far, but I felt sure she was imagining it.

The real trial began in May 1999, when we tremulously rented a three-bedroom villa just below the mountain village of Bellapais, made world-famous by Lawrence Durrell with his book *Bitter Lemons*. At that time there were few houses available for long lets, and with the tourist season about to begin, it was more difficult still as owners could command high prices for the vital summer months that lay ahead. Our bargaining chip, however, was that we would still be there throughout the winter months when tourists were virtually non-existent. The villa was an elderly building, about forty years old the locals told us later, constructed from concrete, flat-roofed and without any of the modern amenities such as central heating or air-conditioning and suffering acutely from rising damp, with draughty windows and ill-fitting doors. It was also filthy. With little alternative, Meryl and I set about stoically to clean everything and make the place habitable. Years of neglect meant that shutters and sliding glass windows had long since refused to shut or to slide and my first task was to remove them all one-by-one and carry out repairs. Internal walls had children's graffiti removed and the floors were given what was probably their first de-greasing and polishing treatments since the house was built. Most of the electric power points had to be replaced and the telephone connections were pure Fred Karno's.

The garden was mature, as one would expect in view of the age of the house. Two huge palm trees stood outside the kitchen, in desperate need of pruning with their dead branches trailing the ground. In fact, in keeping with the house, the whole garden had been allowed to become very untidy and overgrown, and it was impossible to see what it contained until a team equipped with sharp machetes had been sent in. That team arrived in the comfortable shapes of Musa and Osman, a pair of part-time gardeners produced by our next-door Turkish Cypriot neighbour, (Mr) Gazi Bey, who knew them from the village coffee shop.

'Bey', I should explain, is a courtesy title placed after the forename and afforded anyone holding a position of respect in the area, and we were happy to accord him his due. Gazi Bey was what is known as a 'London Turkish Cypriot' and had made his fortune in the UK by manufacturing and selling shoes. Like so many in his

77

position, he and his wife had left the island decades before to escape the economic embargoes set in train against the Turkish Cypriots by the international community's refusal to recognise the country, and to seek work or to found a business elsewhere. Most ended up in north London where even today some 200,000 Turkish Cypriots live and work. Eventually, as their lives improved following years of hard toil, they hankered after a place in the land of their birth, in many cases a holiday home for themselves and their children, usually born and brought up in the UK.

Naturally, Gazi Bey was fluent in English and proved an enormous help to us in our early struggles. He was at that time in his sixties, but of sparse build and wiry. Silver-framed spectacles blended with his thin but all-over silver hair, and his eyes still held a mischievous twinkle. He was a very keen gardener himself and spent hours bent over his lawns and shrubs during long summer visits, usually dressed only in shorts and a battered straw hat. On one particular day, July 20th that commemorates the anniversary of the Turkish intervention of 1974 with a spectacular display of celebration, I watched as, weeding steadily as was his custom in the scorching afternoon heat, he did not look up even once when the mighty F-16s of the Turkish Air Force's elite Red Stars display team screamed and thundered barely a hundred feet over our heads as they regrouped to thrill the more impressionable thronged on the sea front to enjoy the spectacle some two miles distant from us to the north. At certain moments in their display red and white plumes, the colours of the Turkish flag, would trail from the soaring aircraft, leaving huge sickles hundreds of feet high, scything the blue air.

Gazi seemed completely impervious to the sun despite his decades in the gloom of North London, and we watched him gradually tan to a curious tobacco-brown shade over the visible parts of his body as he laboured steadily through the summer weeks. As is typical in much of northern Cyprus, each house is built on a slope, the degree of its angle dictating the layout of the ground floor with differing levels according to the setting-out of the rooms. In Gazi Bey's case, his garden too was terraced and some ten feet below ours where the two properties met. Consequently, whenever he was summoned to negotiate with Musa and Osman on our behalf, he would prop a ladder against the dividing garden wall, shin up it in a trice and vault into our shrubbery, violently shaking greenery indicating where he'd landed. This was all much to our alarm as we feared he could easily miss his footing and cart-wheel back into his flower-beds.

Musa and Osman also manned the ticket office at Bellapais Abbey, probably one of the chief attractions for all visitors to the island. They were great characters and cheerfully set about helping recover the garden. They both loved 'Efes' Turkish beer, the most popular brew available in the north, and its effects showed in their girths. It has to be said how the average Turkish Cypriot is stocky, rarely very tall, and the national diet over the centuries may have as much to do with this as genetics. Musa and Osman enjoyed a quiet smoke too as they pottered about tending and watering the plants. The overgrowth was cleared out using a mattock, known locally as a Çapa, a type of spade but set at right-angles across the shaft. Wielded by an experienced user, it makes quick work of weed growth and tills the soil at the same time. Within a remarkably short period, flowering hibiscus and oleander emerged from the jungle, with multi-coloured bougainvillaea rampant along the boundary fences. We also discovered sweetly scented shrubs of different varieties such as Pakistani nights and the rarer Madagascar nights with its plum-sized berries starting out yellow from the pretty, white flowers, and evolving through red to black. The various jasmines too helped perfume the evening air with their heady scents. Meryl rescued many of the other shrubs, including a beautiful honeysuckle with purple flowers tinged white. She resuscitated the previously hidden herbaceous borders usually containing the ubiquitous geranium together with other hardy and drought-resistant plants, as well as planting many more to enhance our new surroundings. The palms too were carefully pruned back to their tops by Musa and Osman. Edging both sides of the long leaf stalks are lines of lethal spikes that reminded me of the front of a swordfish while the palm fronds themselves have razor-sharp leaves and points like bayonets. Altogether not a user-friendly tree at all, but lovely when safely under control, its teeth and knives out of reach, and the teasing breeze sighing and fluttering through its boughs. Immediately outside the kitchen was a strong frame constructed from scaffold poles that supported a large and mature vine which, after Musa's careful pruning, brought forth a large crop of delicious, sweet grapes while providing welcome shade from the summer sun.

The garden held other delights for us as we were gradually made aware that we were living in a foreign land. Dead-heading some geraniums late one summer afternoon, Meryl saw a movement on the stem of the plant she had just moved across to deal with. About to grab a fading blossom, she realised to her horror that the plant was providing a dozing snake with a comfortable haven for its afternoon nap. With a yell that not only woke up the snake but all residents within a half-mile radius, Meryl set an unbeatable record back to the safety of the kitchen, slamming the door behind her.

An extremely stiff medicinal brandy taken, followed by a more meditative one later, we set out to find in our guide books more information about the island's snake population. It was a worthwhile exercise, as the specimen Meryl almost got on close personal terms with proved to be of the venomous variety. These are the tan or yellow-coloured ones of the adder family, often with lozenge or swirl patterns in a darker hue along the body, which is not particularly long. Bravely, and equipped with a ten-foot pole and a pair of fast plimsolls, I ventured forth to inspect the visitor but it had already vanished leaving behind a tantalising section of the skin it had been sloughing off when disturbed; proof, if you like, that Meryl hadn't imagined it all. Those distinctive, tell-tale marks left by a snake's passage, the twisted scoops in the sandy path, showed the direction of its departure back into the undergrowth. Perhaps, after Meryl's fortissimo scream, it had become like the deaf adder of scripture? Strangely, the locals told us that such snakes are believed to dislike geraniums, which accounts in some measure for the flower's popularity in people's gardens, but this one's mother

81

seemingly had not told her offspring this important fact.

It is said too that the much larger, black snakes can grow to five feet in length with appropriate thickness in the body but are quite harmless despite their fearsome appearance. They were introduced into Cyprus about one hundred years ago in order to reduce the numbers of the venomous ones, on which they feed. Even so, with a more enlightened attitude to all other forms of life with which man shares the planet, both these beautiful creatures are now officially protected. Again, I hope someone has explained the change of policy to the big black jobs.

Shortly after this episode, it was my turn to meet the local fauna, this time in the fascinating shape of a chameleon. He, or she, was walking slowly along one of the low walls in the garden. They are so obviously survivors of the dinosaur age in my opinion, with their rough, armoured coats, serrated spines along their backs, eyes swivelling from the tips of miniature gun turrets as they sweep before and aft in an enquiring arc, while ambling along on thin bowed legs that end in claw-like feet. The miniature dragon's tail literally brings up the rear. He could have sauntered on to the set of *Jurassic Park* and no questions asked.

About 15 inches long overall, he did not seem at all perturbed by my close and impertinent inspection and continued his morning stroll. Knowing their ability to change colour dramatically in order to confuse predators, I was anxious to do something that would bring about this effect. The wall, being constructed of raw concrete, was a sombre grey not surprisingly, but my companion was still arrayed in brilliant emerald green. I coughed discreetly but was ignored and he continued at his leisurely pace. I leaned down a short distance in front of him so that he could not fail to see me ahead. Meryl said this would have turned him green anyhow, had he not been that shade already. Still no colour change, so I concluded much to my lingering disappointment that chameleons don't do concrete.

To continue recalling our encounters with local wild life, there was another incident when Meryl and I were preparing to retire to bed. In fact, Meryl had already gone upstairs. It was autumn, and I was making final checks of locks and switches. As I was about to turn off the kitchen light, I glanced across the room and saw, to my astonishment, a badly damaged ceramic tile just above the work surface which I had certainly not noticed earlier. It looked as though someone had taken a lump hammer to the tile comprehensively smashing it into a huge star pattern. Knowing that no one had been in the place that evening other than us, I was mystified at such peculiar vandalism and moved across to have a closer look. As I did so, I realised with rising alarm that it was in fact a huge tarantula spider, at least the size of my outstretched hand and the largest arachnid I had ever seen outside a zoo or a James Bond thriller.

With its large body mass, dark grey in colour, and from which grew very long, black, hairy limbs, it looked every inch the villain of a thousand horror films. Its bright, beady eyes stared frighteningly into mine and it seemed to be judging my every move. Trembling, I looked for a large glass bowl and thick piece of cardboard to capture it and release it back into the wild outside. Creepily, it seemed to anticipate what I was about to do and, as I started towards it with my equipment, it slid down on to the work top and fell or jumped to the floor with an audible thud, scuttling away beneath the fridge/freezer. The way it moved, and its sheer speed, made the hair rise on my neck. Heroism done for that night, I shut the kitchen door into the hall very firmly behind me, carefully noting its tight clearance with the floor and shot upstairs, hoping that before morning the brute would return to the garden the same way it got in. This particularly alarming event I kept from Meryl as without doubt it would have meant the end of the Cyprus experiment there and then, flights on aeroplanes would have been booked within the hour to take her straight back to Blighty, lickety-split.

Several weeks later we had to replace the fridge/freezer for technical reasons and by agreement with the supplier the old one would be taken away. On the day of the delivery, not unlike Pooh Bear's friend Piglet, I remembered an urgent appointment I had down in Kyrenia and could not be present when the new appliance arrived. Allowing plenty of time for the exchange to take place, I was relieved on returning to the house to find the new machine safely installed, with no reports from

Meryl, still in blissful ignorance of the tarantula affair, of death or injury.

There was plenty of learning to be done too about living permanently in North Cyprus. First priority was to become 'official' in the land which meant visits to the Immigration Authorities and the inevitable forms to be filled in. Passport-type photographs of both Meryl and me were required in quadruplicate for their files. After some enquiries and careful exploration, we managed to find a rare shop where the photos could be taken, in colour, they said. In my case, the lady snapper fitted up one of those silver umbrellas to break-up the full flash, but couldn't reduce the glare bouncing off my spectacles and insisted I remove them. She brooked no argument. The consequent pictures showed a shifty, elderly male with rapidly thinning grey hair, squinting into the camera, eyes practically shut; a pretty unattractive sight I thought, and Meryl said something about having to look at the real thing, specs or no, day in, day out.

Officialdom here tends to be enmeshed in a huge web of red tape and there seemed always to be a large crowd of other candidates doing the rounds with us, not necessarily Brits or other ex-pats. Unfortunately, the local language appears not to include the word 'queue' so what we recognise as a queue is invariably fan-shaped in Cyprus, with Brits politely fringing the outer edges. We were required to hawk ourselves and the piccys around various official departments as part of 'The Immigration Process' and, knowing how touchy some of the 'jobsworths' can be, I got into the habit of removing my glasses when about to encounter someone who might be making careful comparisons between my photographs and me. I am extremely short-sighted without my gig-lamps and, as I stumbled up and down steps, or collided with posts or other people, I was worried that I might come across as inebriated and as such, an unsuitable candidate for a temporary residence permit anyway. Happily my subterfuge went undetected but Meryl said afterwards she hadn't noticed any difference from my normal comportment.

Another part of our induction into North Cyprus included a visit to the main hospital in the capital in order to have a blood test and chest X-ray. To Meryl's outrage, we discovered that the blood test was to ascertain whether we were carrying the Aids virus and, less offensively, the X-ray to check for TB. Hospital visits are a nightmare anywhere in the world, including the UK, and having been given good advice, we had a Turkish-speaking guide to help us through the labyrinth of that particular trial. Although this smoothing of the way cost a modest sum in gratuities, it was well worth the expense as Meryl and I would have stood no chance against the 'queues' or the hospital's arcane procedures. After a week of nail-biting, we were relieved and delighted to learn that we had neither Aids nor TB. Yet another hurdle had been cleared.

Officialdom demanded also a letter from the Bellapais Mukhtar, (the elected head man of the village) who had to confirm that we were indeed living in his area at the address we claimed, and he had to check other particulars too. Accordingly, as Meryl had opted to remain indoors, it being hot, I presented myself at his immaculate home one afternoon and was received with great courtesy. The Mukhtar was a large man, with a thatch of slicked black hair, and dark skinned from a lifetime on the island. He also sported a splendid black moustache. Very bushy eyebrows, also black, protected eyes of almost matching colour. Dark and hirsute, summed him up in a simple phrase. A large hand, hardened from labour, wrapped mine in an eye-watering shake.

As is the strictly observed protocol with strangers in the Near East, the first concern of the host is to offer hospitality, in this case a choice of beer, Turkish coffee or tea. Conscious still of my town-drunk performance earlier in the day, I opted for tea, aware how quickly information passes in small communities. To my great relief, the Mukhtar spoke passable English but asked me to help him put together the letter demanded by the immigration police. He seemed to lay great emphasis on my being married to the lady featured on the other passport, having opened both and spread them out before him for close scrutiny.

He kept repeating, 'You are married?' and looking at me quizzically despite the identical surnames on both documents, and I began to wonder if we really were or whether the Registrar in Hastings had committed some ghastly blunder. I suspect the nervous stuttering and stammering he'd induced in me merely added to his suspicions. Eventually, after a particularly hard stare which I manfully held without further flinching, he seemed to be convinced I might indeed 'be married'. Accordingly, the letter was slowly and painstakingly put together in his large, stiff handwriting, the occasional working out of the spelling of a particularly difficult word being lengthily prompted by me.

When satisfied with the finished result he got up and moved across to an impressive bureau in the corner of his sitting room and after a rummage returned with a small rubber stamp. Evidently the inkpad was not where it should have been and a good deal of heavy breath was exhaled on to the stamp at close quarters in order to coax it to a state of readiness for use. I held my own breath while it was poised over the document for a last quick scan and, as the Mukhtar's official seal was brought down with an exaggerated flourish, I too exhaled with relief.

We moved on then to entering our details in his dog-eared record book, passport numbers and names. Unsurprisingly, perhaps, pronunciation of English names causes the Turkish Cypriots great difficulties and over the years Meryl has become simply 'Mary' and I, to my acute embarrassment when it is called out to me across a street, find I've actually undergone a sex change. The hard 'A' is unknown in the Turkish language and automatically becomes 'a' as in 'add'. But I do not know why they also have difficulty with the 'n' at the end as this takes precedence over the 'd' and slips to the front so, as in some weird anagram, my name dissolves into 'Andria'. All this is quite contrary to the macho image I try to cultivate – hopelessly, Meryl says – and constant, gentle correction does little to change anything for long. So, although spelt correctly, Mary and Andria were carefully entered into the Mukhtar of Bellapais's log. At least we were married.

A small supermarket I frequent on an almost daily basis is irretrievably into 'Andria' but after one visit I forgot to pack all my groceries, leaving some behind. I can only guess someone English who knew me was in the shop emd said something like 'Adrian has left his …..' because the next time I went in faces broke into smiles and everyone began chanting proudly 'Adrian, Adrian, Adrian', like the Chorus in a Greek Tragedy. But it wasn't long before I became Andria again.

The Mukhtar explained how water would be 'on' three times a week for about four hours. Eh? One of the first lessons to learn on a Mediterranean island is that water is precious – up there alongside gold almost. Because of acute shortages, it is scrupulously rationed and something never to be messed about with. One could imagine that village Muktars would unhesitatingly arrange lynching parties should they discover their water is being used or wasted because of dishonesty or carelessness. Even so, this unwelcome news would not go too well with 'Mary' who was used to turning on a tap and remaining totally unimpressed when water flowed out.

The well-established domestic water control system is to mount the main feed for the house in a galvanised metal tank, supported on top of the usually flat roof by iron framework and holding a tonne of water. Immediately beneath this sits an insulated cylinder for the hot water, heated by solar panels tilted southwards to absorb the maximum amount of sunshine. Even in the winter months there is often enough solar energy to supply an average household with its hot water needs. Should this fail through a protracted period of inclement weather for example, most cylinders are fitted with an immersion heater controlled from inside the house.

Ideally, extra tanks, either underground or on the roof, will take in supplies that exceed the capacity of the standard roof tank and provide sufficient surplus water for irrigating the garden. Sophisticated systems incorporating electric motors and float valves can be installed to pump water up and into the roof tanks so that required water levels can be efficiently maintained and managed. Usually, there is enough mains pressure to take the supplied water directly into the roof tanks and of course, gravity gives adequate pressure to all the pipe-work in the house below.

The Mukhtar explained also how the household waste would be collected weekly, provided we bagged it up and put it at the top of our drive early on the appointed morning. One of the refuse collectors from the village was a fine-looking, well-built man with a permanent smile, and so obviously happy to help. He was one of the rare workers who apparently shaved daily, giving his ruddy, full-moon face a sort of polished look. He and I struck up quite a rapport over the months and I would often give him a lift if we met in town or on the way into Kyrenia. According to local folklore the taxi firms in Bellapais bought out the bus rights for the village in order to eliminate competition. As the village is such a tourist attraction substantial income is thus generated for the drivers and owners but the poorer village people have to depend on the generosity of neighbours – or walk. My refuse collector friend could not bring himself to believe that I really couldn't understand or speak Turkish fluently. He would jabber away to me loudly in the car, his comments punctuated with elaborate gestures to make a particular point. Realising sometimes I was not responding to a question he'd asked he would shout even more loudly, in the true English tradition with foreigners. Allowing for my obviously feeble brain he would continue to smile encouragingly to help the socialising along. I was surprised one day to notice he was wearing an old cotton pork-pie hat of mine Meryl had quietly thrown out in disgust and I'd been searching for for ages.

Clutching my letter for the Immigration Authorities with a feeling of great relief, I thanked the Mukhtar for his help and hospitality and bade him a fond farewell, bracing myself to break the appalling news to Meryl about the water supply, or lack of it, as she would surely see it.

In fact, this meeting with the Mukhtar proved to be just the beginning of our troubles with water. On one occasion, shortly after our meeting, despite the supply being turned on at the due times, our tanks remained empty. Musa, as well as being our part-time gardener, and proud custodian of the Abbey, was a bit of a builder also. Most able-bodied men try to take on as many extra jobs as their time and talents permit in an effort to boost their meagre incomes. There is a joke out here that any chap with a hammer is a builder; a screw-driver makes him an electrician and the most basic spanner, a plumber. In many ways this is not so far from the truth as one might imagine; enthusiasm and financial need can lead to exaggerated claims being made for their personal skills.

However, having conveyed our water shortage problem to Musa, he set about cheerfully to trace the fault. At the time, the regular water supply was coming in as scheduled but could be turned off before it entered our villa's system, so the first check point was the inlet from the supply in the road. There was a primitive sort of meter here between the mains and our tanks, so Musa released the unit from its position in the pipe-work and examined it carefully. I should explain how the water everywhere on the island is full of chalk so that lime-scale is formed very quickly – in fact I'd swear one could stand a spoon up in a cup of untreated water. Musa squinted up both sides of the meter, put it to his lips and blew. I reckon he must have the lungs of an old-time South Seas' pearl diver as his breath whistled through with tremendous force. I became aware too, of a sort of mechanical whining sound, rather like a jet aircraft running up in the distance and I caught a glimpse of whizzing, whirring dials on the meter as he held it, and realised it operated with the movement of air as well as water. My heart sank as I began speculating over the size of our next water bill should

Musa have been puffing up the wrong end, and probably setting an all-time record on the island for domestic water charges.

Musa eventually gave the meter a clean bill of health and replaced it so we moved along the pipeline running across the garden and checked each joint as we went up to the house. No problems there. On arriving at the storage tank housed in the carport, Musa eyed the elbow bend where the pipe entered the reservoir and terminated in a ball-cock float valve. I took up a supporting position opposite. He unscrewed the ball-cock assembly and cleared out the lime-scale from its innards with a piece of stout wire produced miraculously from the recesses of his clothing and once more exercised his powerful lungs. Out came the inevitable hammer in its supporting role, a few massive clouts being delivered on the elbow and its connecting pipes. The supply turned back on, we were rewarded at last with deep chuckling and gurgling sounds growing louder by the minute and coming along the pipe. We exchanged knowing smiles and nods. Suddenly, I was struck directly on the bridge of my nose as a jet shot out of the water feed opposite still unencumbered of its float valve. Success of a kind, I suppose. Fortunately, it was a very warm early summer's day, and the shower bath was not that unwelcome. I would just have liked a little more notice. As it was, following a brisk polish, my specs have never gleamed more brightly.

The next trauma in our newly-established household was to be Getting Our Part Load of Personal Effects from the Customs at Famagusta, the main container port some fifty miles to the east. A well-established firm in the UK owned and operated by London-based Turkish Cypriots had sent employees who arrived at the flat in Croydon and carefully packed all our worldly goods into around 75 cardboard cartons, ready to ship to Cyprus. We were warned that the journey, travelling the length of the Mediterranean and stopping off hither and yon to discharge and load cargo, would take several weeks and now the moment of arrival had finally come.

I was required to travel over to Famagusta, meet the North Cyprus-based agent at his office near the docks in the old town, complete the necessary paperwork, talk to the Customs officials, help clear the boxes through and arrange for them to be delivered to our new address. The journey from Bellapais takes over an hour, the most direct route being through the Buffavento pass to the east and across the Mesaoria Plain. The plain is a complete contrast to the Kyrenia area and, once over the pass and down the south face of the mountain range, one enters a different world. As the name suggests, the area is as flat as the English fens, without the water, and the rounded tops of the Troodos Mountains to the south can be seen clearly across the buffer zone dividing the two nations.

Geologists claim that millions of years ago when the planet was still evolving, Cyprus was physically separated into two islands, the Mesaoria plain then being under the sea. In Roman times, the plain was thickly forested with excellent timber, so suitable for ship and boat building that today hardly a tree remains standing apart from magnificent eucalyptuses, well-matured now having been introduced and planted by the British in the 19th Century. However, given adequate rainfall, the plain is the north's bread-basket, and there is no finer sight than the square miles of verdant growth in the early spring months.

The long straight road across the Mesaoria plain seems to go on for ever. The flat landscape on either side drifts past slowly with soporific effect. Devoid of buildings or other features that normally allow the brain to register speed, the buildings at crossroads leading to villages on either side, come as a sudden surprise as one shoots by them. As such, it was a dangerously fast road with many traffic incidents but recent upgrading to a dual carriageway has greatly reduced the number of accidents. Safety is nevertheless reinforced by police vigilance through road checks and radar speed controls. It is worthwhile pointing out here that the maximum permitted speed on 'unrestricted' roads is 100 kph, with semi-restricted areas 65 kph and the urban areas 50 kph. Large clumps of sycamore and eucalyptus rising up from the horizon mark the outskirts of Famagusta, and soon the built-up area begins. A large roundabout decorated with an impressive, once-black but now golden, 'Monument to Victory,' eventually supplies the exit road into the old city.

My business with the clearance agent included a trip down to the docks and an interview with the customs men. As we had come out to retire, our household goods were exempt from import duties, with one or two exceptions. Formalities quickly over, it was arranged for the boxes to be despatched across to Bellapais the following day. On the appointed afternoon, I was astonished to see a small convoy coming up the driveway. First was a substantial truck loaded with our cartons well roped down against the long journey's bumps and pot-holes. Next followed a car containing the agent and behind him, in an official car were two customs officers. My heart sank. It seemed as though we were in for an extremely lengthy and tedious few hours while officialdom trawled through each box and examined everything, including my socks and handkerchiefs and probably Meryl's underwear.

The cartons were lifted off one by one and stacked by the front door. As the weather was fine and dry, no problem with that. Meanwhile, the customs chaps had disappeared from sight. We continued the unloading and with half the stuff lying around the garden they returned. The customs man with the greater quantity of shoulder braid asked me whether we had a television set. I suspected a trap here because I already knew that the TV system in Cyprus was different from the UK's, so had deliberately not brought our old set, knowing we would have to buy a new one and we'd had it for some 16 years anyway. I admitted having a computer though, a retirement gift from my company as an expression of their pleasure at my departure. No, that was fine; but was I sure I hadn't brought a TV set? Of course I was sure, but kept my irritation to myself. The customs man seemed to be as fixated on TV as the Bellapais Mukhtar on marriage. Eventually, I think he believed me and asked for two or three particular cartons chosen at random to be opened. While we were doing his bidding, he and his companion disappeared again. I raised my eyebrows to the agent, who nodded towards the side of the garden that overlooked the sea in the distance. Both men were staring over the pine trees and olive groves as the land fell away to the north and the coast. We joined them to say the boxes were ready. The chief one said in immaculate English, 'My grandmother is buried at Limassol and I haven't been able to visit her grave since 1974'. This struck me as a bit of a *non sequitur* and hardly germane to the business in hand but I did not wish to intrude on private grief. Nevertheless, I could not for the life of me work out how we'd jumped from TV sets to his late-lamented relation, sorry though I was about it as he looked sad enough to blub at any moment. Feeling like the Dairymaid with the King, I resisted the temptation to pat his arm and say 'there, there', but it was difficult. Fortunately, he seemed to come out of his reverie of his own accord and business was resumed with no TV set discovered and my much-prized computer remaining of no interest whatsoever. So, that was that: another hurdle overcome, and we could start unpacking and making the house feel like home at last. And, incidentally, nothing was broken when all had been sorted out – not even a chipped cup or a cracked saucer.

CHAPTER VI
CATS

We had been in the house for only two weeks or so when Meryl noticed a young cat appearing from time to time amongst the dense garden foliage. It was before Musa and Osman had waded in with the weaponry, and the garden, still six feet high in over-growth, would have concealed a charging tiger closing on you at forty miles an hour, let alone a cat. In Cyprus, one doesn't have to go out looking for a cat; they find you. Even if you're not too keen on the idea of adopting one, and in our case we had just passed on our Croydon cat to the kind lady who bought our flat and were in no hurry to take another under our wing, they seem to have an uncanny knack of judging exactly when you'll run out of half bricks thus knowing when it's safe to move in.

Word must have travelled quickly through the cat population of Bellapais that the Fleetwoods, lately arrived from England, were a soft touch and all you have to do is to turn up looking pathetic. Panda, as he became in view of his white fur and rather appropriate markings, had been awarded a diploma with distinction in that field and within a disturbingly short time was rejecting the proffered tin of inexpensive cat food in favour of leftovers from the family supper table, and if that be salmon steaks, Icelandic cod or roast beef then that was fine by him. The understood pact between Panda and us was that we would feed him and he would keep out or down things that crept or crawled over the messuages, as our lease described the property and its gardens. We had been told how many Cypriot cats will skilfully tackle snakes and know exactly how to grab them before getting bitten.One tended to take this folklore for granted as it would require the skill, patience and resources of a David Attenborough to prove this one way or the other.

Nevertheless, Panda rushed through the door early one morning looking as though he'd been in the ring with another cat, one obviously formed in the mould of a feline Mike Tyson, head swollen and eyes puffed up in the most alarming way. After a brief examination, I decided that he was probably suffering from toothache, and rang our charming local vet.

Dr Türker arrived forty minutes later and declared that Panda had suffered a snake bite in the throat (the twin wounds made by the fangs were clear to see once Türker lifted his head up) and was on the point of handing in his feeding bowl for good. Suspecting this possibility, the good doctor had brought along a couple of stiff doses of anti-snake serum and, while I held the poor creature, banged 'em both in. Typically, I was on the receiving end of Panda's wrathful reaction and collected a couple of searing lacerations on the forearms as a touching sign of gratitude. Fortunately there is no rabies out here so I managed a swift recovery.

It took a couple of days for the cat to regain its composure and within a week his confident swagger had returned, although his vocal chords were apparently affected as he seemed to quack rather than miaow. He became understandably jumpy for a while and preferred the middle part of any patch of bare soil or terrace so that, presumably, he couldn't be easily surprised. We shall never know whether he attacked the snake or vice versa.

An unwanted addition to the four-legged strength appeared about six months after Panda settled in, in the form of a small ginger cat. In the intervening time, the garden had been cleared and one could see what and who was entering and leaving from the many windows around the house. Since his acceptance, Panda had conscientiously kept his side of the bargain and, being a 'full-male tom-cat', had the build and attack stamina to defend his territory to the maximum and did so efficiently. The ginger job was a puzzle. I had tried to shoo it off but it simply lay down and miaowed pathetically in the standard, prescribed manner to extract the most sympathy. Playing my trump card one day, I collected Panda and, unkindly perhaps, placed him about three metres away from the unwelcome visitor, making sure they were in clear sight of one another, and waited for the fun and games to begin.

To my displeasure, Panda stared at the newcomer, its full ginger coat indicating that it too was a male, sat down and began cleaning himself. I recited the appropriate section of his contract to him from memory but it had no effect. Ginger smirked at me and also sat down to enjoy his triumph and the autumn sunshine. I remained perplexed, but Meryl was taken with Ginger's pretty colourings. They were beautiful scrolls of pale caramel on deep bronze, the patterns perfectly book-matched on either side. The design changed on his legs and tail to neat alternating rings right down to the paws and tail tip. I had to admit, I did quite like him, apart from a slightly camp and mincing walk, deeply unattractive when viewed from the rear. So, that was it; I was beaten game,set and match.

As we now had two resident cats, we felt it best to take them along to the vet to have them checked over and possibly to get them 'seen to'. There are cats aplenty in Cyprus and we shared the general view among Brits that we should do our bit to help control numbers by having pets neutered. Along we trotted, only to discover Ginger was female! This explained, of course, Panda's reluctance to beat the living daylights out of her as uncharitably requested by his master. To reduce our embarrassment, the vet too was surprised and told us that only one ginger cat in a thousand was female. Why should we be so lucky? Well, at least that accounted for her unfortunate walk and I felt she could henceforth be excused this defect when we had company round.

In due course, both cats were 'done'. In Toffee's case, however, the vet found little to remove as her ovaries had not fully developed, which may have had something to do with her sexual orientation problem. I should perhaps also explain that Toffee was so-named not only because of her colour, but just as much for her adhesive powers when firmly seated on one's lap. She has that, to me, rare ability to treble her natural weight when someone is trying to remove her from a surface she prefers to remain on, and can go into a special rigid mode that makes it almost impossible to get the necessary grip underneath her body.

The following spring, when the days were lengthening and the sun was just beginning to reach into the sitting room again, I descended sleepily one morning to set about making the tea. Habitually, I checked the sitting room as we would leave one of the glass doors slightly ajar so that the cats could come and go in the night. With a rented villa, fitting an orthodox cat-flap was not an option, and my encounter with the tarantula had put the lid on that idea for all time. On entering, there was Toffee, shoulders down, rear up, tail curled conveniently round to one side in the shape of a question mark, her back feet performing dainty dance steps, as one of the ugliest toms I've ever seen was locked in a close embrace with her. I had no need of the question mark, knowing only too well what was going on. Toffee was singing and purring to herself at the same time, so a charge of rape could not be brought. Her friend was one cat to whom Meryl and I had definitely not been introduced; a tabby by colour, but with an iffy eye, a couple of unevenly sawn-off ears and a lascivious grin on his lop-sided face. I was shocked and scandalised and all but broke my umbrella prising them apart. After the verdict of the vet, I could not understand this worrying upsurge in Toffee's libido, and wondered whether Meryl and I might yet find ourselves grandparents again in a few weeks' time. As it worked out, all was well, and I put it down to the unquestionably smooth talk and charm of the tabby and a slight aberration on Toffee's part but the whole episode was most distressing at the time.

Not long afterwards, a Welsh family we had become friendly with asked if we would take in and look after their 7-year-old son's canary, as they had to return to the UK for an extended period. Somewhat reluctantly, in view of the two resident cats, we agreed, so 'Tweety Pie' was duly installed in a spare bedroom amidst high security. An elaborate safety system was evolved and implemented to keep out curious four-footers. After all, it was not the likelihood of the cats catching the bird so much as frightening it to death. Meryl became very fond of the new arrival and put herself in charge of its well-being.

One early lesson learnt was the need to place a dark cloth over its cage at night. Forgetting early on in the proceedings, we were awoken while it was still almost dark one summer morning as Tweety Pie joined lustily in the dawn chorus going full swing outside, with a song belted out at somewhere around 100 decibels. After a while though, he began to play Meryl up, no longer seeing himself obliged to behave as a guest in a stranger's home but feeling free, it seemed, to act as the hooligan he really was beneath his polished feathers. His favourite trick was to broadcast seed husks together with his droppings in a 360 degree arc, with the range of a metre all round, despite the various guards designed and fitted to prevent just that: the vacuum cleaner was feeling the strain and beginning to object. Most fun of all was Tweety Pie's bath time when Meryl insisted on providing a generous dish of warm water. The subsequent scene reminded me of Trafalgar Square's fountains on Boat Race night and we were greatly relieved when the owners returned to claim him.

Our first Christmas in North Cyprus

Early December 1999, and our thoughts turned to the Christmas festivities. We had begun to feel that something was missing; the long-drawn-out pre-Christmas hype that begins in the UK around the end of September. Nothing. But then, of course, this is a Muslim country and December 25th a normal working day if it falls between Monday and Friday. We were a little surprised to learn that the Cyprus 'weekend' was the same as ours, a legacy perhaps of its time within the British Empire as well as the secular week introduced in Turkey by early in the 20th Century when Friday was declared no longer their day of rest. So Saturdays and Sundays became natural rest days. Charmingly, the many Turkish Cypriots who have lived in London for any length of time are very much into Christmas, with decorations in the home, including trees and bunting, presents in stockings, mince pies, Christmas cakes and puddings – and turkeys. The Muslim religion recognises Jesus anyway as a prophet, and his name is inscribed with others including Abraham, Isaac, Jacob and Moses around the inside of the dome of the Mosque of Oman in Jerusalem, (the Dome of the Rock) built in the 6th Century on the former site of the Jewish Temples.

The manager of our regular shop stopped me one day early in December and asked whether we'd be interested in a 'fresh' turkey, farmed and fattened locally, and due to be ready shortly for the festive table. On arriving home, I reported the good news to Meryl who, after some mental calculation, announced that one around 5-7 kilos would be just the ticket. I placed our order accordingly the next day. Smiles and nods confirmed that all would be well and I waited to be told when the bird was ready for collection. A week before Christmas, with perfect timing, the management declared our turkey had arrived. I watched greatly alarmed as a fit-looking young man emerged from the storeroom, struggling slightly with a massive bird, and plonked it on the check-out counter, panting hard. When it was placed on the weighing machine, the mechanism shot off the Richter scale. I suggested, with faltering confidence, that this could not be our bird as we'd ordered a much smaller one. Ah, but these birds, each of a similar size, were all that had been sent.

In a confused mental state, I parted with a substantial fortune as the young Samson placed the brute in the boot of my car with my other heavy shopping. I should perhaps explain that my car was at that time a very simple Nissan Sunny, imported from Japan. Yes, I know. But these models were used and driven in Japan for the first two years of their lives. After that time, all motors must undergo an MOT of such a high standard that it is unattainable without spending money disproportionate to the value of the vehicle. The Japanese motor companies, with full cooperation from the government, know exactly what they're doing, and the unfortunate owner has little alternative to buying a new car. Thus does the industry keep bowling along. In the UK I was fortunate enough to have the use of a company car but that turned into a pumpkin when I left and we had deferred buying our own until we reached Cyprus. At that time, 1999, the government here allowed retiring ex-pats to purchase a car locally without paying import duties, and we had taken advantage of that privilege. Given that the car was already two years old as well, it was not very expensive. As everyone knows, the Japanese also drive on the right side of the road as opposed to the wrong side, so it was suitable for our new island home.

I should have realised something was not quite right about the turkey when, having added its weight to the rest of my shopping, it caused the rear suspension to sink on to its rubber stops. My little Nissan Sunny is a car I love, with many sophisticated features such as air-conditioning, electric windows and mirrors, automatic gearbox and front-wheel drive. I readily concede it has little if any 'street-cred' but pretend I'm not too fussy about such things.

On this occasion, it was the front-wheel drive that threw in the towel. I became aware of a certain amount of slippage as I went to move off. The sound and smell of tortured rubber suggested that wheel-spin was hampering our forward progress, with the bonnet higher than usual and the boot sounding suspiciously as though sparks might be trailing from its bottom. It felt like a speed boat without the speed or the water. Panic seized me; I pulled into the kerb and telephoned to the War Office. Stammering out the story to Meryl, I could tell things were not going well at the other end of the connection. I had to agree with her; the bird was ridiculously large for two people and we would, as she put it, still be eating turkey sandwiches in May. I was told very simply to return to the shop and, despite all the excited anticipation of a fresh turkey, opt for a smaller, frozen specimen.

Fortunately, the shop management cooperated happily. They expressed their apologies again for failing to provide the smaller turkey requested. Everyone helped riffle through the cold cabinets to find some suitable alternative. Eventually, only one solitary turkey was discovered; a modest job about the size of a large thrush, and brown with freezer-burn. On Christmas Day, Meryl and I shared a meagre four slices of breast, and threw a sinewy leg to each of the two resident cats. Henceforth, Meryl announced, she would be taking Christmas lunch only at hotels or restaurants.

About two years after this event, we discovered that one of our favourite restaurants, *Le Jardin* in Ozanköy, was offering a special Boxing Day luncheon. It featured a cold collation of viands from which one served oneself, together with a marvellous choice of pickles and chutneys, bubble and squeak, and mashed potatoes; exactly the change one needed after the traditional Christmas fare. The lunch became so popular that one had to book by October in order to get a table. The second year we took with us two of Meryl's girlfriends, a cosy foursome. Just how cosy, I was about to discover.

There is an old joke about the conjuror's trick; don't blink or you'll miss it. I can only think I must have blinked – metaphorically, that is.

Suddenly, I found the ladies were not only discussing ailments and operations, but had become aware that some years ago I'd had a problem with my prostate gland requiring surgery. Inexplicably this information seemed to shoot like wildfire into that part of the public domain surrounding us. One of our companions asked me, none too discreetly in my opinion, how this had affected my sex life. Stuttering and yammering incoherently, and feeling my cheeks mantling to a deep pink, I realised that other conversations in the crowded restaurant had hushed to whispers while it seemed all those present were eagerly awaiting my response. My voice by now a shrill falsetto, I tried to shift the emphasis of the discussion to the delicious cheeses on offer or the homemade trifle. My interlocutor persisted. 'Have you tried Viagra?' she enquired. You could have heard a pin drop. No more boring stuff about the hideous vase Aunt Lottie had sent over as a Christmas present; this was Adult TV coming to life. Patting my hand consolingly, the well-intentioned lady, en route for a holiday in England the following day, loudly promised to bring me back some Viagra and at this happy outcome, our fellow diners seemed content and resumed their meals and conversations.

As things subsequently turned out, the lady was away so long that she obviously forgot her offer and returned without the Viagra. Meryl was hugely relieved, having already declared that on its receipt she would be locking herself in her bathroom and swallowing the key.

On the subject of medical matters, it is worthwhile relating how Meryl experienced some acute stomach discomfort a few years back that, after many visits to doctors, followed by scans and blood tests, turned out to be caused by gall stones, and extremely painful for her. Fortunately, we took the precaution of taking out special overseas' insurance when coming here so medical treatment could be carried out as necessary without the fear of huge bills suddenly overwhelming us. As each year passes, there seem to be more and more private medical clinics and hospitals springing up, all of very high standards in terms of qualified surgeons, medicine, nursing care and hygiene. Even at that relatively early period in health development in the north, we were directed to a private clinic in Famagusta where Meryl was examined by a sympathetic practitioner who suggested keyhole surgery. Hitherto, the removal of a gall-bladder meant a huge scar and a month in hospital, whereas he reckoned she should be out again within 48 hours at the most. And so it turned out to be. Many of our British chums were astonished at learning that such advanced surgical techniques were so readily available in North Cyprus at that time. Although it took a while for Meryl to recover completely, it seemed no time at all to me before her left jab and the fast following right hook were as sweet as ever.

CHAPTER VII
ELECTRICITY

For the interested reader, one has in all honesty to draw attention to another challenge to the resident living in North Cyprus – the electricity supply. To say that it is subject to cuts from time to time is like saying that Monday follows Sunday. It would be too boring to set out a critique on the north's electricity generating system but it does come under pressure when demand is excessive as when in cold weather too many customers switch on heaters or air-conditioners in the hot months. Sudden storms or violent lightning strikes can cut supplies in an instant, and the established settler learns to stock up on candles, matches, torches, batteries, lamps and gas mantles, ready at all times for such emergencies.

Some of the sudden summer storms around Kyrenia can be extremely dramatic, with terrifying flashes of forked lightning and thunder that is ridiculously amplified by the mountain range. Shortly after we arrived to live here, we were treated to one performance of such intensity that I half expected the Angel of Armageddon to appear in the middle of it and put the trumpet to his lips.

Naturally, from time to time electricity maintenance work has to be carried out, sometimes to change the cables to a thicker gauge in order to conduct greater loading into an area where several new buildings have been occupied, or to increase the capacity of a sub-station for similar reasons. It is everyone's constant cry that we are never given adequate warnings of protracted cuts when the authorities plan to work on the system. If the job is long and more difficult than they expected, the power can be off for 18 hours or longer, no joke in hot weather and the freezer packed full to bursting.

One time, however, in early January, our weekly English newspaper published a notice announcing impending cuts covering a wide area, including where we lived, while structural changes to the network were being carried out on the next day, Sunday. Huzza! we thought in our household – at last, a proper warning, and appropriate action could be taken before the event. Thank goodness I had not decided to de-frost the freezer.

Because our fax machine and cordless telephone both turned their faces to the wall and went to sleep without the stimulus of electricity, an inexpensive telephone that works independently of the supply was purchased and duly connected. After all, several members of the family in the UK sometimes like to ring at the cheap rate on a Sunday.

An alarm clock was set for 5.30 on Sunday morning so that the immersion heater could be switched on well ahead of the given 7 o'clock deadline. No slothful lounging in bed on that day of all days. The washing machine too was loaded and set to work, again in good time to allow for its job to be completed before the shutdown. So far, so good. But, as the hours ticked by, the catastrophe did not befall us. Had there been a mistake over the names of the towns and villages affected? Surely not, as the list was endless, with only Sodom and Gomorrah missing. So there the mystery remained, with full power available all that day without a second's interruption and for several days thereafter.

The next Saturday, however, our household was plunged into electrical paralysis at 7 o'clock prompt. No immersion heater on for showers, no kettle for that vital first cup of tea. etc, etc. Cravenly leaving Meryl to her moping (why, somehow, is it always the male's fault when we are caught entirely unawares?), I went into Girne to do some shopping. Amongst my purchases was the weekly paper announcing extended electricity cuts for, yes, that very day! Terrific. At least I found it quite romantic drifting around the house by candlelight that evening, feeling like a serf in "Pride and Prejudice", but my wife refused to co-operate with a *décolleté* frock and candelabra, citing hot wax as the reason. Despite the best efforts of the lads on the wires and switches to get us back for longer than two minutes at a time, it was 10.30pm before the 21st Century returned. Alas, too late for the electric blanket to do its stuff so it was not easy either coaxing madam into an icy bed. I was reminded of a female version of the Michelin man, swathed in extra clothing to the point of invisibility, including thick socks and a woolly hat – very uncuddly. The paper issued an apology afterwards, pointing out that it had printed the warning in good faith but had not been informed of the last minute cancellation of arrangements before publication, nor of the revised date.

Whenever Meryl pops back to the UK to visit her family, she likes to seize the opportunity to buy things not available out here. On one such trip in early summer it was mosquito nets, manufactured in Taiwan and purchased from that emporium known as Ikea. Naturally, on her triumphant return bearing these prized trophies, I was appointed to fit them, one over our bed, the other in the spare room. First, the nets have to be parted from their substantial packaging and laced around a sort of spacing ring some eighteen inches in diameter, the whole then being suspended from a large hook fitted in the ceiling whilst standing on the bed. It looks and sounds easy but believe me, I felt as though on a bouncy castle with attitude. One must look plain daft, swathed Miss Faversham-style in acres of swirling white tulle while dancing like a demented dervish in order to locate the hook, which has evilly concealed itself against the also-white background of the ceiling.

Eventually, of course, with patience, skill and much swearing, the net frilled amply around the state bed in the most gratifying manner. On discovering that it had only one entrance I was told to set it at Meryl's side. Waking in the night in response to a call of nature, and alarmed at the imprisioning yards of fabric, I spent some frantic moments fighting deperately to escape its determined clutches. That apart, we slept that first night with windows thrown wide, inhaling lungs-full of welcome, cool mountain air. But what a rude awakening in the morning as we scratched away. There on the inside looking out was a considerable number of mosquitoes appearing well fed, relaxed and contented. Meryl and I on the other hand appeared to be in the terminal stages of measles.

I can only assume that in Taiwan the mossies are large four-engine jobs and no match for the nets whereas our local lads are slim and agile, able to fly at will in and out of warp and weft. A major strategic re-think was soon underway and, for once, I didn't get the blame.

CHAPTER VIII
JOINING THE COMMUNITY

As Meryl and I settled into life in the area, we met many more British ex-pats and after a time decided to join the Anglo-Turkish Association, set up some years before with the worthy objective of furthering relationships and understanding between the two cultures. It proved a worthwhile exercise and that first year we took part in many of the trips and lectures they organised.

Most interesting of all for us was an early October weekend in the Karpaz region, which we never got round to visiting on our own holidays. The plan was to join the ATA's chairman Harry, and his wife Kate, in their large 4-wheel-drive jeep, as the roads at that time would have proved too much for my humble Nissan Sunny with its thin tyres and suspension designed for sedate city roads. We set off in convoy with about eight other vehicles, Harry leading the way. We had planned to take the north coast road that leads from Kyrenia through to the village of Kaplica, cross over the land end of the Karpaz and take lunch at a restaurant in the village of Büyükkonuk.

Although it has been recently upgraded and straightened out, tourist maps of the north used to take enormous cartographic licence with this coastal road, showing it as winding gently against the sea with the odd bend from time-to-time. The reality was a continuous wriggling snake of a track as the dozens of ravines leading from the mountains to the sea had to be negotiated by turning inland for a distance, depending on the ravine's depth, and returning after the inevitable hair-pin bend, to the coast. As already noted, we drive on the left here still, which added considerably to the excitement of this journey. Driving east, one is on the outside of the road, nearest the sea and cliffs, with oncoming traffic better protected on the land side. Add too, the ingredient of lorry drivers who leave the matter of safety in the hands of Allah, and I believe the adjective to describe this part of the journey, is 'hairy'. Fortunately Harry is a very phlegmatic character, a former racing driver and immune to panics at the wheel, unlike the writer who perpetually screams abuse at every transgression perpetrated against him when driving, a founder member of Road Rage. A brief stop for morning coffee half way along this dizzying journey allowed us to catch our breath and to admire the unspoilt views over mountains and the dazzling coast line we'd just traversed. The nearby sea just below the café pounded dramatically on the rocky shore as if in unison with the turmoil on the road above.

We travelled on, the forbidding fortress of Kantara glowering high overhead as we began to move inland for the last time. The passage across the top of the peninsula was tame by comparison and far more relaxing for the passengers, who could afford to release their vice-like grip on any solid part of the vehicle they felt could be trusted. At the village of Büyükkonuk, the convoy was met by Lois and her husband İsmail who live there. Lois is a most interesting lady in that she is Canadian by birth but married and settled with her handsome husband in this village where his family relocated from the Paphos region after the troubles of 1974. At the time of our visit his 95 year-old mother was still alive and working at her loom. The party enjoyed a typical Turkish lunch in the local tavern called, appropriately, the Sultan. Being a somewhat larger party than the village would normally expect, many of the inhabitants had arrived to help get drinks and to prepare and serve the food. This made for a friendly, family atmosphere with everyone talking and laughing together outside in the fine, warm and sunny weather, shaded under a spreading vine, heavy with fruit – perfect Cyprus!

After lunch, it was time to look around the village, something Lois and İsmail had been at some pains to organise. We were led on a conducted walking tour. I should explain how Lois had completely immersed herself in the life of the village, spoke fluent Turkish and with İsmail, had brought up their three children there. They were determined to do everything they could to foster the old village traditions and prevent them from dying out as they have in so many other villages. İsmail has constructed a special studio outside their attractive house, which he also built himself, and there the villagers can offer for sale their products – fabrics and rugs, the famous and beautifully delicate Lefkara lace; carved wooden dolls and toys, and bottled honey and olive oil.

They have helped keep the village olive mill going and, as it was the right season, we were able to see it at work. Noisy and terrifying machinery was whirring round, huge electric motors driving thick belts that ran up to centrifugal pumps and pressing machinery, all without EU-regulation protection guards. A Health and Safety inspector from the UK would have swooned on the spot and, after resuscitation, closed the place down immediately. However, the villagers had been pressing oil in this way for decades and knew exactly what they were doing. The olive crop has to be picked by hand and the locals bring in tubs and buckets to wait patiently until their turn comes to pass them over to the mill workers. Apparently, it is up to the owners of the olives being pressed to say to what extent they want their crop to be crushed. Too much, and the pressing will be bitter and useless, and contaminate the rest of their oil. Again, with years of experience they seemed to judge it exactly.

Next, we were taken to a village house where its elderly resident was weaving rugs in her front room. Lois explained how this small, nimble-fingered lady was from an isolated village in Anatolia in Turkey, and even Lois had difficulty understanding her regional dialect. I find it fascinating to study people and their characteristics and this lady, with her oval-shaped face and fair skin still as smooth as an eggshell, seemed to me to be from Mongolian stock and I wondered whether her ancestors had stayed on when Gengis Khan returned to the homelands. When planning this event, Lois had called on her to make the arrangements and, in response to her question asking when we would be coming, replied 'in October'. The old lady seemed puzzled as she turned ver this information in her mind. After a while, she looked up at Lois and asked,

'What's October?'Lois revised her information, 'At olive time'. With understanding dawning, she nodded and smiled happily.

Meryl and I were interested in some of the rugs already finished in the room and asked Lois to enquire the price of one we particularly liked. It was colourful and, Lois told us, woven to a design the weaver had learned as a child at her mother's knee. Amazingly, these people go out into the fields to gather wool from the sheep's backs, wash and spin it, and then find certain herbs and other plants in the hedgerows and woods from which they extract dyes. The finished fibres are then used to produce these wonderful rugs with bright colours that look natural because they are. Lois reported a sum in Turkish Lira, which I converted mentally to £50. Unprepared for the need for so much Turkish money, I proffered a £50 note. The old lady examined it contemptuously. There was no need for words as her facial expression and body language said clearly that she was a bit too long in the tooth to fall for a gag like that from someone she'd never seen in her life before. After all, £50 worth of Turkish Lira is a very thick bundle indeed at then 1,500,000 to the £ and, as for the offer of a single, solitary foreign note, well! Pull the other one. Lois, noticing my discomfiture, kindly came to the rescue and managed to convert the sterling into 'real' money from the shop's till. Today, the rug looks perfect in my study and serves also as a reminder of this charming interlude in our Cyprus story.

Harry was, and still is, Chairman of the British Cemetery Committee in Kyrenia. I should explain how there are no funeral directors as such out here, as the Muslim Turkish Cypriots are buried quite simply in a shroud, according to their tradition, usually within 24 hours of death. Even today, the British Community in the north is reckoned to be around 6 or 7000, although the precise number is unknown as there is no compulsion to register with either the British High Commission in Lefkoşa, or the British Residents' Society, the latter being a purely voluntary organisation established to help residents and would-be residents and to provide appropriate information about living here.

This organisation was one of the first societies to be set up by the British in North Cyprus. It has always fielded a strong and dedicated team at committee level with UK-experienced specialists in administration, finance, welfare contacts, social activities and those who have become adept at liaison with the TRNC Government. Over the last few years, the BRS has flourished under the exceptional chairmanship of Julia Price. Her sheer professionalism and communicating skills have been outstanding and, on a point of principle, she has attended a great number of charitable events held in the north – and there are very many indeed, with a lot being annual fixtures – as well as funerals. Julia and her team have also organised countless fund-raising activities, always giving freely of their time and energies, and have raise tens of thousands of pounds for local charities.

This reminds me of a story told to me recently concerning the chairman of one of London's most prestigious advertising agencies. He was extremely outgoing as these chaps usually are; tall, distinguished-looking and always immaculately dressed in Savile Row suits, showy silk ties and hand-lasted shoes from Lobbs. He was proud of his voluntary chairmanship of a large old people's home outside London and made a point of visiting it most Saturday mornings to spread a little cheer. On this particular occasion he was walking down a long corridor and greeting as he passed many of the residents with whom he was already familiar. Coming slowly towards him on a Zimmer frame was a rather stern-looking elderly lady he had not seen before. 'Hallo! Hallo!' he boomed amiably, 'do you know who I am?' Without the slightest pause in her progress, she snapped back, 'Ask Matron; she'll tell you'.

The Cemetery Committee is also formed from volunteers in the British community. Needless to say, ex-pats do die and are usually buried locally, with very few being repatriated to the UK; only sometimes for cremation as there is no crematorium on the island, north or south. There are two British cemeteries in Kyrenia, the original one that was opened in 1878 when the British first arrived in Cyprus and is now full, and the new one on the east side of the town. Digressing for a moment, the old cemetery near to the big 'Lefkoşa roundabout' on the Kyrenia by-pass is full of interest to the historian, with many British residents from the Colonial era resting there. Most intriguing perhaps, are four graves of soldiers from the Black Watch, stationed on Cyprus during the early days of British Rule. One of them is the grave of

Sergeant Samuel McGaw, VC, who 'died on the line of march to camp Chiflik Pasha of heat appoplexy [*sic*], 22nd July 1878, aged 40 years'. Sergeant McGaw's VC was won on the field of battle during the Ashanti Wars. In St Andrew's Church in Kyrenia there is a set of four small brass shields presented by the Black Watch, commemorating all these brave men.

As Meryl and I became absorbed, as it were, into the community I was approached to join the Cemetery Committee and, although I was rather surprised, readily agreed. Perhaps word had got round that I owned a dark suit, look permanently sad and walk with a measured tread. Curiously enough, although being initially approved by the Committee, official membership has to be confirmed by no less a personage than the British High Commissioner himself, at that time Mr Edward Clay. Within 2 days of agreeing to join, I received a letter from him endorsing my appointment. Clearly, his feet did not match his name.

The service we can provide is limited. There are no hearses or limousines and it is not possible to conduct any part of the funeral involving the coffin in the church of St Andrew's, but only at the graveside. Three or four male members of the Committee will proceed in a suitable vehicle, taking a coffin from our store with them to the mortuary where the body is lying, either in Kyrenia or Lefkoşa – always the latter when a post mortem has been ordered by the police. The body is placed in the coffin, which is then sealed and taken to the prepared grave where it is lowered to await the burial service, conducted usually by the Chaplain of St Andrew's.

Harry told me once how many people settling here cannot resist the temptation to re-invent themselves. Shortly before Harry took over the chairmanship, the committee was called upon to bury an elderly Englishman whose widow was insistent that his memorial stone should contain details of his decorations, qualifications, awards and insignia. Some instinct prompted Harry to make checks in the UK and he discovered that none of the claimed titles was genuine.

Another story concerns the burial of a pukka military gentleman bearing the rank of General. He had served with great distinction in the Second World War and the local paper was at pains to produce a fulsome obituary. To begin with, it described the General as 'bottle-scarred' producing howls of protest from his friends. In an attempted correction the following week, he was referred to as 'battle-scared' after which the paper sensibly withdrew from the fray.

Shortly after taking office, I was told how all members of the committee were invited to the High Commission in Nicosia to attend celebrations for the Queen's Birthday, held usually in early June around the time of the 'Trooping the Colour' ceremony on Horseguards. Going along with Meryl for the first time, I was astonished but delighted to see among the generous refreshments on offer two complete drums of Stilton cheese ripened to perfection and to which one helped oneself, together with nearby piles of suitable biscuits and crusty bread. As Stilton is virtually unknown in the north, let alone available, I'm afraid I got rather carried away and Meryl found it necessary to hide in the shrubbery with embarrassment. With grim satisfaction, Meryl pointed out the following year how there was only one Stilton, carefully guarded and served sparingly by a large Greek Cypriot lady who was definitely not to be trifled with.

CHAPTER IX
THE KYRENIA MOUNTAIN RANGE

Much has been written about the Kyrenia Mountains. The maps suggest they run in a fairly straight line for almost a hundred miles, but to stand somewhere along the shoreline, say to the west of Kyrenia town at the new ferry harbour, and look south, one sees that they are in fact set in a beautiful curving arc, their strange, uneven serrations moving rhythmically along the tops and descending gradually in height as the eye is drawn east into the Karpaz where they finally disappear beneath the sea towards Lebanon.

Thrillingly, there are to be discovered no fewer than three ancient castles, now in ruin, but still clinging to the loftiest peaks in the chain. Rising steeply behind the narrow coastal strip, the highest points are over 3000 ft above sea level and many of the loveliest villages sit in this ribbon of fertile land between the sea and the foothills, thus enjoying perfect views over water to the north and the rocky slopes to the south.

These castles of St Hilarion near Kyrenia, Buffavento a few miles to the east and Kantara at the land end of the Karpaz peninsula have their origins in the mists of Byzantine times but were further developed in the 12th and 13th Centuries. Built as they are on the tops of the mountain range, they slip into the skyline as though they might have grown out of the rock. It is said that they were intended as strongholds to keep watch on the coast and to warn of raids from the north, the direction from which trouble usually arrived. As each is in sight of the next, the proven system of fire beacons was used to send quick news of impending attack. Kantara would pass a signal to Buffavento which is in clear view of the capital, Nicosia. To the north, Hilarion too was in view of Buffavento while Kyrenia castle has clear sight of both strongholds as Hilarion sits almost immediately above the town. Thus the northern communication chain was secure and complete.

By the time of the Venetian occupation, however, the whole system of warfare had changed and they saw the old fortresses as redundant and partly dismantled them, so that in the event of a local revolt or an attack on the island going against the defenders they could not be used by an enemy. Kyrenia castle, thrusting its battlements into the harbour mouth, was remodelled to take into account the recently introduced weaponry of heavy cannon. A new bastion built to face a threat from the sea was constructed with a rounded surface, tapering gracefully upwards so that ship-launched cannon shot would mostly ricochet off any part of its wall, while much of the castle was extended and reinforced around with massive masonry. Imprisoned within the resulting tight embrace is a small but charming chapel probably dating from the 12th Century and well worth the visitor's time in seeking out.

In Lusignan times, during the 13th and 14th centuries, Kyrenia castle incorporated a royal palace the remains of which can still be seen once inside the large courtyard. But in the long summer months the fortress in the harbour was considered too confining, dusty, and stifling in the heat so the court moved up to St Hilarion castle to enjoy the cooler mountain air. There the favoured few settled in their extensive summer eyrie built on three distinct levels, and an engineering marvel of the age. Slotted skilfully into the mountains at almost 2500ft above the town, the palace offered them a much more comfortable and fresher proposition with its gentle mountain breezes drifting through the rooms and courtyards throughout the lazy summer days. Huge cisterns built on the outskirts of the castle walls collected vast amounts of winter rain so that water was abundant. Mules laboured up the mountain each day from the town to bring provisions.

Although in decay now, St Hilarion was obviously a place of great luxury in its prime, with a beautiful belvedere that caught the slightest zephyr and offered spectacular views over the dramatic coastline as well as the adjacent jousting field where, to alleviate the boredom of inactivity, the knights, mounted on their pampered and gaily caparisoned horses, tails dyed scarlet, demonstrated their prowess with the lance.

The castle walls flow freely over the steep mountainsides and at the corners lookout towers are built at the very edges of dizzying chasms in the splintered rock fissures. One of these towers is named after the Lusignan Prince John, brother of King Peter I and co-regent with

Queen Eleanor, prior to Peter II attaining his majority. Suspicious and easily manipulated, John was falsely convinced of the treachery of his Bulgarian bodyguards and had them lured individually into the tower on various pretexts, seized and flung to their deaths on to the rocks hundreds of feet below.

Found in the middle ward or section of the castle are the remains of a beautiful small chapel, its decorative columns constructed from alternating red brick and stonework courses, the triple-lighted window in the traditional semi-circular apse at the east end opening on to a fabulous bird's-eye view towards the Karpaz. According to legend, the original building occupying the site was not much more than a weather-proof cave inhabited by a hermit known as Hilarion, a 10th Century holy man who is said to have spent his last reclusive days there, and after whom the castle was named.

At the topmost section of this fortress, reached by long stretches of roughly-hewn and uneven stone steps, are the now roofless royal sleeping quarters, but even today the view westward from the ruined 'Queen's window', as it is known, is breathtaking as it looks out along the curve of the Kyrenia mountain range to the extreme western edge of the island, where it dips into the sea at Cape Kormakiti, some thirty miles distant. (PLATE 10)

It is said that many years ago, Walt Disney was so taken with St Hilarion castle that he used it as the architectural model for the palace when making his classic film 'Snow White and the Seven Dwarfs.'

In the great mountain forest fire of June 1995 parts of the castle were severely damaged and the former Great Hall in the centre section, converted long ago into a restaurant for visitors and featuring a wooden floor and roof, was completely destroyed. In 2005, however, renovations to the castle were completed and, as well as the new refreshment room, some chambers have been roofed over and decorated, and set out with life-size models to depict clothing and fashions as well as furnishings from the Lusignan period.

With some notoriety for its gloomy past as a prison as well as a stronghold and look-out spot, Buffavento castle is presently the most neglected of the fortresses. It is the highest of the three and its name means 'where the winds blow' and for anyone who has been to the top and gazed over the north coast, there is no need for further explanations. One cannot help but marvel at the sheer skills and determination required to build a full-sized castle at such a lofty and remote spot. The place is reached by a 4 mile track from the Buffavento Pass coming along the south face of the mountains that brings one to a parking spot at the foot of the steep footpath leading to the fort. There, next to a solitary olive tree, is a memorial to the crew of a plane that crashed into the north facing side of Buffavento Mountain in the eighties as it approached Ercan Airport. Tragic though this accident was, it was fortunate that it was not carrying a full load of passengers. The climb up the zig-zag path takes around 40 minutes, going at a steady pace. Despite

129

looking quite terrifying when viewed from below, the ascent is not as vertigo-inducing as one might imagine, and again the views to the south over the Mesaoria Plain as one gains height are lovely and invite regular and welcome pauses to enjoy them to the full.

After the Venetians rendered the castle useless for military purposes, there is disappointingly little to see apart from the guardhouse at the entrance and some rooms on the way up. The climb to the final section is not for the faint-hearted as it involves a series of steep steps with a daunting precipice on one side guarded by a wobbly handrail (now, happily, made secure) to help give confidence. The first time I ventured up to see Buffavento, a severe thunderstorm was gradually developing. As I was making this final ascent, it suddenly seemed a good idea not to hold on to the metal handrail in view of the regular and blinding lightning flashes around my head. Equally disconcerting as I kept climbing were mountain goats rushing down past me in some fright. However, the view from the topmost ruins is truly stunning. On clear days one can see for many miles; Turkey, a suggestion of the eastern Mediterranean coastline on very clear days, and most of the North Cyprus coastline in great detail. Fascinating too, is the way that sounds are carried up the escarpment over considerable distances. A fishing boat, for example, chugging its way out to sea can be heard clearly, engine popping as it pushes through the coastal currents, and the sounds of voices from the villages can add intriguingly to the aural mix on a calm day. Some traditions claim that Emperor Isaac's daughter, having fled here at her father's instructions, surrendered herself and the castle to the

Lionheart when he progressed this way after taking the island. (PLATE 11)

Considered the most romantic of the trio, Kantara castle is the last in the eastward line but perhaps the best sited to afford the finest views. From here in the winter cold, a lucky few have seen the snows on the mountains of Lebanon. Kantara can be reached from many directions as evidenced by the meeting of five roads in the centre of the nearby village named after the castle. There is the inevitable cafe in this small hamlet – a welcome find after what is usually a longish journey. A further short drive from this point leads through a narrow pine forest and soon brings one out near the main entrance to the castle. Where Kantara differs from its two brothers is its unique and delightful situation. Relatively lower than the others at 2000 feet, it sits astride the land end of the Karpaz and, at such a height, both Famagusta Bay to the south and the open sea between Cyprus and Turkey to the north can be seen curving away far below. Three of the four sides of Kantara sit on the edges of what appear to be sheer rock faces falling away into abysses all around. Again, it is a triumph of medieval engineering. Some towers and battlements remain in comparatively good condition although, as with the others but less so, much was made ruin by the Venetians. One tradition claims that it was to Kantara that Emperor Isaac was brought after his capture by Richard. (PLATE 12)

As well as the castles on the Kyrenia range, there are many monasteries well worth exploring, on both sides of the foothills. However, it should be noted how several of them are now enclosed within Turkish army camps and inaccessible to visitors. One that it is possible to visit is the Antiphonitis monastery in its beautiful setting and fairly close to the Alevkaya forest station from which it is sign-posted. Sadly, from time to time the monastery suffers from the unwelcome attention of vandals but the authorities try desperately to preserve what they can by keeping the building locked, the key being lodged at Kyrenia castle. However, requests to see the place are sympathetically received and, on some days lately, a warden is present. Uniquely now in Cyprus, the church has a large central dome supported by eight alternating piers; four built into the wall and the other four free-standing. The church is also noted for its wall frescoes and another of Christ Pantokrator on the underside of the dome. At one time, beside the monastery, stood a grove of the last remaining liquid-amber trees to be found in Cyprus.

As hinted earlier in the narrative, Bellapais abbey is the historical and architectural jewel of the north and claimed by some architectural historians to be the finest Gothic building in the Levant. It was built by the Lusignan King Hugh lll in the early 13th Century and was called locally the 'White Abbey' because of the colour of the monks' cloaks but its name 'Bellapais', corrupted from the French, means literally 'beautiful peace', which it doubtless enjoyed when first consecrated. It was reputed to have been presented with a fragment of the 'True Cross' early on in its existence by a French knight who in return asked for masses to be said for the souls of his wife and himself. The abbey has known its troubled times too. In the late Venetian period, just before the Turkish invasion of 1571, scandal broke out when it was discovered that many of the monks had taken mistresses and only their male children were allowed to become novitiates – nepotism in a word. Ironically, when the Turks arrived, they sacked the monastery and thus signalled its rapid decline into desolation and decay.

Happily, there is still enough of the buildings remaining to suggest its glorious past and today it is considered the perfect romantic ruin with the broken tracery of its cloister, roofless chapter house and monks' dormitory above also open to the skies but still equipped with each monk's bedside cupboard cut into the stone wall, and his window. Although but a sad shadow of its past, the chapter house still features some delightfully carved corbels from which sprang the long-departed roof ribs, and well worth studying up close. The original church at the south side of the building is also contemporary with the abbey but was handed over to the Orthodox Church in 1571 when the Ottomans invaded. Because it was in daily use until 1974, it is still in a marvellous state of preservation. It is said to contain the grave of King Hugh III, the abbey's original founder .

Reckoned as the finest part of the abbey remaining and also in fine condition is the monks' former refectory with the Lusignan royal arms, together with those of Cyprus and Jerusalem, beautifully cut into the pale grey marble lintel over the main entrance. The north wall, heavily buttressed and with six large windows overlooking the sea, is built up from the rock escarpment below to a total height of some 90 feet, this *tour-de-force* achieved by its medieval masons being seen to best advantage from roads beneath the village. Within the thickness of this massive limestone wall is a narrow staircase, leading up to a small, fretted pulpit corbelled out from the stonework and from which one of the monks would read suitable texts from the Bible to the others while they ate in silence. Again, to our shame, the British used this building as a small arms shooting range, the marks gouged in the stone wall at the east end still testifying to this act of sacrilege. Today, the refectory is used for all sorts of concerts with singers and musicians claiming that the accoustics there are almost perfect, quite fortuitously, whether for orchestral performances, string quartets or choral singing, and all artists greatly enjoy performing there for that reason.

Beneath the refectory is a stone undercroft originally used by the monks as their victual store for the abbey, recently cleaned out and refurbished and used now for smaller concerts or recitals and other events such as art exhibitions. There are many other abbeys and monasteries in the north – the large one of St Barnabas has already been described – while others have been converted into hotels of a kind such as that of 'Anastasia' in Lapta to the west of Kyrenia. As noted in the account of the church in Karaman, a great number of the Greek churches were badly damaged because of fighting during the intervention and several of the ones in better condition are used today as icon museums. It is best to refer to the official guide books for fuller details about them all.

CHAPTER X
CHARACTERS IN KYRENIA

We were introduced quite early on after our arrival on the island to another British couple, Robin and Maryon, who live in Sherwood House, (their joke, not mine) in the village of Ozanköy. Maryon was a principal ballerina with the Royal Ballet and a young contemporary of Margot Fonteyn and Moira Shearer. Maryon retained her international fame as a teacher of ballet and this second career, like the first, took her all over the world for many years after her stage performances ceased. Indeed, on arriving in North Cyprus in 1989, Maryon wasted no time in setting up the Maryon Lane School of Ballet where she patiently taught young Cypriot children the elementary skills. In their charming house there are many souvenirs of Maryon's dancing life, including several framed ballet programmes from Covent Garden, with her on the same bill as Nureyev, and one to celebrate the Centenary of the Royal Opera House in the presence of the Queen and Duke of Edinburgh. My personal favourites, though, are the portraits drawn of Maryon by Osbert Lancaster, the most delicious caricaturing her when dancing as Pineapple Poll–huge eyes and a sailor suit. Just wonderful! Another original, by Ronald Searle, shows her dancing as the Dairymaid in *The King's Breakfast*.

When we had dinner with this delightful couple one evening Maryon entertained us with some of her reminiscences. The one that amused me most occurred during a performance of *Giselle* at Covent Garden. There is a moment in the story when the principal ballerina (not her on this occasion) makes a Peter Pan-style flying exit on a wire into the wings, at a dramatic and emotional stage of the ballet. At this particular performance, she arrived with a little more force than usual and caught the 'catcher' off balance. Moments later, an astonished audience was treated to the unusual spectacle of this beautiful and elegantly costumed ballerina swinging back into view, but this time entwined around a startled stagehand. The burly lad, obviously taking due cognisance of the considerable heat backstage, was clad in the union-negotiated uniform of string vest and mooning jeans, a long earlier career in Her Majesty's Services evidenced by a liberal covering of tattoos on arms and torso. It brought the house down.

Robin proved an interesting character also. In 1930, his father was a pilot flying out of the old Croydon airport and used to be frustrated by regular delays caused by fog at many times during the year. Once airborne he would notice how, when he was flying south and clear of the London area, the ground below him around Red Hill was completely clear of fog or mist. Deciding one day to explore further, he motored down to investigate this region and discovered a very large farm with abundant flat land attached, in a place called Gatwick. He was pleased to note also, the presence of a railway station and a race course in the area. With financial help given reluctantly by his own father, Robin's father managed to buy the farm and from it started a small private airfield, almost always clear of fogs. The rest as they say, is history, and Robin still has a published booklet recording these early events and the development of Gatwick Airport over the past decades. Fascinating too was the fact that, when developed by later owners in 1936, the small airport featured a central passenger disposal area with radiating tunnels that could be moved mechanically along rails toward the waiting aircraft, thus keeping departing passengers fully protected from inclement weather.

Sadly, though, dad was a bit of a lad and a series of personal problems meant that the airfield had to be sold on in 1933, even before Robin was born. However, personable as Robin was, he managed to gain a place at the RMA Sandhurst and made the army his career. As with many of the retired ex-pats in Cyprus, Robin was happy to find something to do during the long days and, at the persuasion of his chum, one Allan Cavinder, discovered he had a natural talent for hosting and running a bar. For several years he assisted others but eventually found a place that he could manage himself. This was at the Meadow Garden restaurant on the outskirts of Kyrenia where he reigned supreme, building up a large clientele with whom he and Maryon still keep in touch although the bar had to be closed after Robin's heart surgery some years ago.

One of Robin's favourite yarns – and he has many – was about Winston Churchill. According to Robin's account, when Churchill was planning his funeral he purposely stipulated that the train bearing the coffin to its final resting place in Bladon churchyard, Oxfordshire, should leave from Waterloo although it was obviously a difficult train journey from there to the north with Paddington being the natural point of departure. Churchill's reason was to compel General de Gaulle, who Churchill knew would feel obliged to attend the funeral, to travel to Waterloo. The two war-time allies always had a tense and difficult relationship. Churchill used to contend that the heaviest load he had to bear during those long years was the 'Cross of Lorraine'.

Robin's former bar partner, Allan Cavinder is, like Robin, a Yorkshireman. Allan was in Cyprus considerably before the 1974 intervention and was an eye-witness to that momentous event. Allan kept a detailed diary and has written a great number of accounts of those times for newspapers and other media. The local English language weekly paper in the north, *Cyprus Today*, has also published many thrilling articles written by Allan, describing what ex-pat life was like in those whirlwind days of 1974, when Turkish troops arrived to rescue the beseiged Turkish Cypriots. The British government sent the aircraft carrier HMS Hermes to take off beleaguered British ex-pats, but Allan was one of the few who refused to leave.

Allan Cavinder was originally from Hull in the East Riding of Yorkshire, a town as it was then, where my family moved for a short time during the war, principally because my father was sent there to help fight the King's enemies. Also, coming from Portsmouth in Hampshire, we were pleased to be farther away from the German Luftwaffe, one of whose favourite targets was the Royal

Naval Dockyard. My brother and I sang as trebles in the choir of St John's Newland in Hull, and one of the perks was a half-crown for singing at weddings, a much coveted sum of money for small boys in those days. On meeting and chatting to Allan's second wife, Joan, in Kyrenia one time, she and I calculated that my brother and I had sung at her first wedding in St John's in 1948. Not a line one can get off many times in life! One is frequently reminded in North Cyprus what a small world it is.

I am surprised by the number of people living here who are from Hull. There is Hilton Moses, for example, whose family were funeral directors, his grandfather having set up the business in the 1870s. Appropriately, Hilton is a member of the Cemetery Committee here too. Some other friends, David and Jeanette Burton, lived originally in Swanland, the delightful village just to the west of Hull and favourite haunt of the old-time trawler skippers. Jeanette was treasurer at St Andrew's church for a time. Jean Clark, who has kindly provided the photographs for this book, is an Hullensian also.

On my short journeys to and from Kyrenia, I got to recognise many of the locals who would walk everywhere. The normally good village bus services did not operate to Bellapais as noted earlier, the story being that the taxi drivers had clubbed together to buy the bus franchise and then banned all public transport. The road up there from Kyrenia, some three miles distant, becomes progressively steeper as one nears the village. Because Bellapais and its abbey are practically a World Heritage

139

site, tourists flock there, but have to use either a hire car or taxi. Not very satisfactory for the poorer villagers who are obliged to seek lifts from kind neighbours – or walk.

One such character was a shepherd who pastured his goats up in the mountain foothills or in the fields around the village. Like many of the villagers, his weekly treat was a shave at one of the several barber's shops in Kyrenia, where he seemed also to do the daily shopping for his family. If we met somewhere in the town on foot, he would greet me warmly and kiss me on both cheeks. I must say, this took some getting used to. Unshaven for several days usually, and habitually carrying around the distinctive aroma of goats, it proved quite an ordeal. He had a limited repertoire of English and we would converse on the same topics regularly. It could be confusing; he would ask how my 'mammy' was and I could never pluck up courage to tell him she died fifteen years before, as the enquiry was kindly meant, I felt sure.

One day when I bumped into him he was accompanied by a lady whom he introduced as his 'Mammy' and I was astonished to see how relatively young she was. Obviously, life as a shepherd out in all weathers was tougher on the body than I had imagined. After a time though, I twigged that 'mammy' was his English word for 'wife', so matters became clearer after that. This information I kept from Meryl who I knew would not f eel flattered to be known as my 'Mammy'. I gave him a lift back to Bellapais one lunchtime when he was carrying a large plastic bag. He was always keen to show me his purchases and this turned out to contain around 2 kilos of fresh sardines, no doubt caught that morning and probably bartered from one of his fishermen friends for goats' cheese. We chatted in our normal fashion and I dropped him off. As he got out of the car, I noticed a puddle on the carpet and realised the bag had been leaking. For weeks after, the car reeked like Billingsgate Market at the end of a particularly long and busy day, much to Meryl's disgust.

There seems to be a barber's shop on every street corner in Kyrenia and for a while I couldn't understand why so many. Then the local tradition of the weekly, or twice-weekly shave suggested a greater demand than for only a monthly short-back and sides. For many years while living in the UK, especially as a young man, I used to wonder about the significance of the legend 'Singeing' engraved on old-fashioned barbers' shop windows, but never thought to enquire about it. In Cyprus, I quickly found out its significance. Without so much as a by-your-leave, the barbers here will at some stage in the haircutting procedure, twist a small piece of cotton wool around a wire, and dip it in a bottle containing some kind of clear liquid. Taking out a cigarette lighter, they touch-off the wool which ignites with an alarming 'whooshing' sound, shake off the excess inflammable liquid and apply the leaping flame freely to one's ears and cheek-bones. The sudden and over-powering reek of burning hair – and one suspects there's flesh in there too somewhere – accompanied by crackling sounds is disturbing to put it mildly. Suffering as I do though with wax build-up in the ears, I half imagined that a little fortuitous melting as a result of the process might also be taking place, but perhaps this is too fanciful.

Musing further on this new experience, I found myself wondering whether the practice might have crossed the Atlantic years ago and if so, whether our American cousins had dropped the middle 'e' as they have the unfortunate habit of doing with such words, leading inevitably to the formation of the Barber's Shop Quartet. Incidentally, while on this subject of the dropped 'e' in America, growing older is bad enough, but can there be an uglier word than 'aging'? And if you use 'routing' to mean planning a way to somewhere, how do you describe cutting grooves in timber?

Not suprisingly, perhaps, there are several Welsh families living in the north and like the Scots and Irish – we have them too – they like to celebrate their Patron Saint's Day wherever they are in the world. Consequently, throughout the year, restaurants here advertise special celebrations of Burns' Night, St David's Day, St Patrick's Day and St Andrew's Day in sequence and with appropriate national foods to help set the mood. Jeff Iverson is a Welshman but limits his patriotism to supporting the Welsh rugby fifteen. He has a wonderful fund of stories and related a true one I found particularly entertaining, although it does not feature a Welshmen. It concerned a German prisoner-of-war interned in a camp on the Isle of Man. From the time of his capture, he worked very hard and conscientiously at his escape plan, which was to seize a boat in Douglas harbour and make his way back to the Fatherland via Ireland, sympathetic always to the German cause. He made a passable military uniform, mostly from old blankets and he even made badges to support the story that he was Polish and therefore didn't speak any English. Over several months he secretly excavated a short tunnel under the barbed-wire fence. On the night of his escape attempt, he was standing at the roadside when a lorry carrying Welsh soldiers into Douglas stopped and gave him a lift. He successfully passed himself off as a Polish soldier and his hospitable new friends insisted he spent the evening with them. Evidently, the regiment's hospitality was generous with the result that the German was dropped off drunk some hours later, at the exact spot where they picked him up. Sensibly perhaps, he decided to go back into the camp and try again another time. Needless to say something similar happened on each of the several occasions he tried to get away. Eventually he gave up his escape plan altogether and settled for the odd night out with his new-found friends of the Welsh Regiment.

Many years later, Jeff met the German in Berlin where he had become a sound recordist for a German TV crew. He still spoke no English, but discovering that Jeff was Welsh, insisted on plying him with drinks explaining through an interpreter how Jeff was the first Welshman he had met since his Isle of Man days and he wished to say 'thank you' for the warm Welsh hospitality he had received there.

Incidentally, Jeff is a former programme maker with the BBC where he was a staff correspondent and later a television producer. Today, he is very protective of the Turkish Cypriot cause and writes compelling articles from time-to-time for the local weekly newspaper. One such piece for *Cyprus Today* gave an account of the 1974 massacre of Turkish old men, women and children by Greek fighters. This occurred at the village of Atlilar as the Greeks were fleeing from the advancing Turkish army. Thirty-seven villagers were rounded up, including terrified infants and babes in arms, then shot dead. Earth was rapidly bull-dozed over the bodies by Greek Cypriot villagers. And there were other Turkish villages also targeted for mass murder that night. Atlilar is commemorated by a beautiful stone garden of remembrance around the mass grave site and is to be found just a few kilometres inland from the entrance to the ruins of Salamis. Jeff believes strongly that visitors to the north should be encouraged to visit Atlilar. On glazed display boards at the grave site are contemporary reports of the atrocity culled from the world's press, ranging from the *London Times* to the *New York Times*, thus countering attempts by the Greeks to deny their genocidal crimes.

I am lucky enough to have an excellent dentist in the old Turkish quarter of Kyrenia. She is a youngish Turkish Cypriot but was born and brought up in London. Her parents believed passionately in education and gave her every encouragement to study and to develop her career. She trained at Guy's Dental Hospital, still recognised as one of the best in the world. I find her delightful company–an unusual sentiment when discussing dentists. Also, as an added bonus, I've never before had one I could kiss on greeting. Because of her London upbringing, Aysen feels more British than we do and frequently says when talking about the irritations that can be imposed by the locals. 'They're not like us, Adrian'. And yes, she can pronounce my name correctly.

As one ages, visits to the dentist become more frequent and of longer duration and I am not exempted from this. Well into the time when crowns are the only satisfactory long-term solution to my dental problems, they are what Aysen spends her time and my money on. On one visit, she was examining an old crown rather critically and announced that she didn't like it. It was too big, ugly and badly made: she decided it had to go and set about removing it. With my mouth seeming to contain most of the implements in her surgery, it was difficult to argue or to take part in the discussion at all so I had little opportunity to object as she set to. Unfortunately, it turned out to be more securely in place after 20 years of service than the Queen's after 50 and she resorted to an impromptu session with a miniature hammer and chisel. Quite a novel experience...

Our Bulgarian cleaning lady speaks just a little more English than we speak Bulgarian. This leads to some confusing and tricky situations at times. Antiseptic cleansers for the bathrooms, for example, were used freely on brass and silver alike, a fact realised when we could not understand why the once-gleaming surfaces assumed a grey and fuzzy appearance. After a time, we realised that the chief problem was that her most uttered expression was 'OK' and, when we were attempting to explain some request, OK would be her inevitable response. Thus falsely reassured, we would lapse back into apathy believing she had understood, only to find the job undone when she was ready to leave.

145

Despite countless exhortations and explanations conducted mostly in sign language, she could not get the hang of our vacuum cleaner but her efforts with the machine provided some fascinating viewing for the unreconstructed voyeur in me. Around forty years old, the lady has enormous and beautiful breasts, left unfettered during the hot months and thus allowed complete freedom of movement beneath her thin summer t-shirts. Consequently, I find that as with those Renaissance portraits, my eyes follow her around the room. I'm afraid that at 68 I've become just the sort of bloke I used to detest when I was 34. Such distractions prevent me from becoming too angry when she knocks chunks of plaster off the corners of the rooms and passageways as she hauls the Hoover about the house. As well as these wonderful personal assets, the dear lady is extremely conscientious and works hard under all conditions without close supervision. She is completely trustworthy and we happily leave her in charge of the house when Meryl and I go out together, hoping that most of it will still be standing when we return.

There is a strong contingent of Pakistanis in the north of the island and they too are very hard-working and honest. As such, they are immensely popular with the Brits and eagerly sought after to work as gardeners, cleaners and general handymen. Our gardener, Ali, has been resident on the island for over 20 years and is famed for his industry and personal integrity. However, even after such a long time in the company of English people, he has a style of speaking the language that is all his own. Many sentences need to be dismantled and reconstructed before comprehension dawns. For example, soon after he began working for us, and on checking a young palm that didn't look too healthy in one of our terracotta pots he asked Meryl, 'Dying this one why?'. I have got used now to the challenging mental exercise of listening to what Ali says and, in culinary style, stirring up the words and adding a verb.

Quite recently, Ali recounted an experience he had early on in his time here. He was gardening for a Turkish Cypriot, married to an English woman. The house was new then and the garden barely established. As the growth of the lawns, shrubs and trees began in earnest, the husband decided to find a donkey to eat the grass as an attractive 'green' alternative to a noisy lawn mower. A donkey was duly found and enclosed in the large garden area late one afternoon. When Ali turned up for work early the following morning, he stared in disbelief. The garden was unrecognisable with almost all the flowers gone, including the roses, shrubs and trees nibbled down to bare stems, but the lawns were entirely untouched. So taken aback was Ali that he went out of the garden into the road to verify that he was indeed at the right house. Later the same day, the donkey was returned to Güzelyurt, whence it came, and the lawn mower re-commissioned.

To everyone's delight, some Pakistanis have opened restaurants, and it is a great treat to have genuine Sub-continent food, with many of the herbs and spices used coming here direct from their country. No one enjoys a curry more than the average Brit these days, so at the height of the tourist season it is virtually impossible to get a table at any of these places unless bookings have been made a few days before.

Another addition to the restaurant scene was 'Both Worlds' in Çatalköy, a village about two miles to the west of us and very popular with Meryl and me. The British couple who ran it specialised in Thai food and were so determined to make it authentically that Des and Lyn would often spend their winter break in Thailand where they worked in local restaurants to learn more about recipes and their ingredients. Usually they returned with plants from which they successfully grew many of the herbs and even spices they needed for the special Thai dishes. One evening, we took my younger sister Angela and her husband Trevor there during their holiday from the UK. After the usual very pleasant and varied types of meal we all sat replete outside on the terrace enjoying our complimentary drinks from Lyn and Des. My brother-in-law went off in search of the gents' only to return a few moments later looking ashen-faced and shaking slightly. Apparently, he had inadvertently knocked against an oil lamp fixed to the wall for use in the event of a power cut, and dislodged it. It fell on to the lavatory bowl immediately below, smashing both, thus rendering the loo beyond use for the remainder of the evening. We were all mortified and I took Des quietly aside to explain how Trevor was Hampshire County Council's number two solicitor and not some leather-clad biker from a Chapter of Hell's Angels bent on trashing loos up and down the UK's motorway network. As it was, Des took the accident in good part but we had to endure watching a procession of staff filing in and out with assorted cleaning equipment to clear up the broken bits of china and glass. The final embarrassment was a large hand-written sign, hurriedly erected on the now-locked door to the gents', proclaiming 'OUT OF ORDER'. I'll say it was. Angie and Trevor had come in their hire car and left shortly after this incident while Meryl and I stayed on to reinforce our concerns with the proprietors. In fact, among his many talents, Des is also a builder and told us he would be able to replace the loo easily the following day. Nevertheless, a substantial tip helped spread a little oil on this troubled water and eased our consciences. On the way home along a back road, I too felt the need for a quick leak and popped behind the gate to a field. Meryl said I looked disgustingly like a French lorry driver relieving himself after lunching on two dozen moules and a bottle of Sancerre. I retorted, somewhat truculently, that the ladies' hadn't been destroyed so she was fortunate to be able to scoff.

One of Kyrenia's finest attractions is its splendid lending library, housed just behind the town's main Post Office. Open every Wednesday and Saturday between the hours of 10.00 and 12.00 it offers thousands of books. Again run exclusively by volunteers, it charges a low annual rate to its members and one can take out as many books as one wishes without the fear of fines for lateness in returning them. Holidaymakers too can gain access to the library's large stock by applying for short-term membership, costing only a few YTL, to cover their time here. The library is also home to the 'Kyrenia Society' and its chairperson, Anne Hughes, organises a week-long annual trip to the Turkish mainland to explore its many historical treasures and sites. Competition to participate in this eagerly anticipated event is fierce to put it mildly, and the waiting list for the next one often opens before the last year's trip is over.

Two other favourite characters of ours are Martin and Ahmet who jointly own and operate the 'Neptune', a wooden-hulled boat they keep moored in Kyrenia's old harbour and use for day trips along the coast. Martin was born in South Africa and speaks immaculate RP English whereas Ahmet is a local man, but English-speaking just the same. They bought the 60 ton vessel some years back as almost a wreck but set about stripping it down to its oak ribs, and fitting it with a huge diesel engine suitable for its weight and purpose, while gradually building up the planking and super-structure in the form of an 18th Century galleon. In the saloon, there is a collection of fascinating photographs taken at various stages of the ship's meticulous restoration and one can readily understand why she is now reckoned the safest ship afloat in Kyrenia harbour. To reinforce her swashbuckling appearance, Neptune flies the Jolly Roger from her mizzen mast. As well as the regular trips up and down the coast, she sometimes makes a special voyage of some two or three days, sailing steadily eastwards and rounding the tip of the Karpaz to enter Famagusta Bay. Guests enjoying these trips are accommodated at night on the decks using either the benches built in to the sides of the hull or in their sleeping bags. Of those who have been on this voyage, many say how wonderfully needle-sharp the night sky is with the entire absence of artificial light at the far end of the Karpaz. A resident cook is aboard on these occasions, usually Suzee, who is an expert caterer and professional supplier of provisions to the hungry. Suzee's marvellous food is supplemented by the heroic efforts of Martin, ever-present behind the bar. On all Neptune's jolly jaunts, there are stops to allow swimming from the boat via a gangway let down the side and there can be nothing quite as refreshing as a dip in the cool, clean sea on a broiling hot day. Oddly, to me at any rate, the intensely high summer humidity is only rarely present over the water and many tourists and ex-pats seek refuge on boats offering trips from Kyrenia harbour as a welcome respite from the acute discomfort on land. (PLATE 13)

No holiday to the Kyrenia area could have been considered complete without a visit to the Green Jacket Bookshop. Owned and set up by Bryan Balls, it derived its name from Bryan's time in the Green Jacket Regiment and the shop was freely modelled on the Waterstone'plan of dark green walls and shelves. Sadly, however, even as I write, Bryan is retiring and the shop is closed now. As the name indicates, the place specialised in the sale of books, both new and second-hand, and provided a service for the ex-pats completely lacking in the area hitherto. But Bryan was happy to sell other articles to extend his range to the resident Brits and visitors alike with such things as maps, postcards, and paintings produced by the locals. It is extraordinary how many artists there are around practising in water colours, oils and pastels, many of them at almost professional level. With a wonderful sense of humour, expressed in his rich Harrovian chuckle, Bryan is a much-loved character. Known by everyone, he has helped and encouraged a great deal of talent in the Kyrenia district. There are several locals, both ex-pats and Cypriots, who specialise in the production of greeting cards, calendars and decorated paper for writing letters or notes and Bryan sold these items for them too.

Shortly after setting up the bookshop Bryan received what must be described as a poison pen-letter from the Greek side criticising him for his actions, the general tone somewhat threatening. Green Jackets don't scare easily however and Bryan wrote a scathing reply, signing it contemptuously 'Balls'.

One talented Brit has produced a marvellous booklet of walks in the north. As well as detailed sketch maps of the suggested routes, there are descriptions of interesting features, buildings and views to be seen on the way. So popular is the publication it is now in its fourth edition with new walks being added or revised each time. Quite recently, another group of enthusiasts has set up a guided tour company to escort walkers along the beautiful Kyrenia Mountain range. The customers are taken up the mountain by 4-wheel drive vehicles, dropped off with their guide and collected again at the end of the trek. This too is proving increasingly popular, especially in the spring and autumn months when the climate is at its best.

Bryan Balls whom I got to know well over the years, has a fund of fabulous stories to relate most of which have his audience in stitches as he is a brilliant raconteur but many, unfortunately, are not quite suitable for publication. He was stationed on Cyprus in the 1950s, when the EOKA troubles were getting into their stride. But that is not to say the troops here had no fun. One of Bryan's recollections I treasure most concerns an incident at this time when he was caught on a beach with a young lady, *in flagrante delicto,* also in Her Majesty's Service. The young lady's female commanding officer demanded an interview with Bryan to explain his behaviour. As Bryan says, there was little one could add to the eye-witness's account, but the irony is that the lady CO, now retired and in her eighties, was still on the island until recently and regularly visited Bryan's bookshop. Hardly liking to refer to it himself, he often wonders whether she remembers that earlier, rather awkward meeting...

While we're still in uniform, as it were, one of Bryan's regular visitors to the shop in search of military books was a chap called Jim, formerly a Corporal of Horse in the Life Guards. Fine-looking and softly spoken, Jim was a natural gentleman with his quiet manner and lively sense of humour. It was always good to see him enter the shop and the three of us would enjoy some ribald leg-pulling together. It was Bryan who told me one of Jim's best stories. Some years ago, Jim was deputed to run the bar one winter's evening in the Guards' Officers' Mess when a visiting dignitary was the guest of honour. It was proving a convivial night when the whisky ran out shortly after coffee and liqueurs had been served. His C.O. already in fine fettle, called Jim across; 'I say, old chap, just pop out to the village and fetch another couple of bottles, would you?' As politely as he could, Jim explained that it was snowing hard, the village was a good mile or so distant and he, Jim, was wearing only a short-sleeved cotton shirt and lightweight trousers. 'Of course, of course! Quite right! Take my coat and hat and orf yer go, dammit!' Jim duly donned the C.O.'s greatcoat and cap and set off. At the gate, Corporal Jim was handsomely rewarded for his pains with the sight of his mates falling in at the double and snapping to the salute as he strolled past. Not for them the luxury of asking their Commanding Officer why he should be going walk-about on his own in foul weather and at that late hour. Jim, alas no longer with us, never told us whether his colleagues ever found out the truth.

Around the middle '50s, according to Bryan, a local scandal attracted much attention. A bachelor Duke of the British Realm arrived in Kyrenia harbour aboard his yacht and stayed throughout the long, hot summer. During the season he enjoyed a wildly romantic affair with a beautiful young English girl who, unfortunately, was already married to a local Turkish Cypriot. When the time came for His Grace to depart for England, the lady watched distraught as the yacht was prepared for sea but, as the boat moved out through the harbour mouth, she could bear it no longer. Throwing herself into the water she swam out to the craft, was hauled aboard by the crew and carried off in triumph to become a Duchess. Her unfortunate husband, rather peeved at this turn of events contacted the Duke and sought compensation for his loss. The Duke, being wealthy as well as in love, readily agreed and passed over a sum that beggars belief for the time. Suffice it to say, it set up the former husband in great style for the rest of his life.

I have always been interested in engravings, old maps and views of places long vanished under the march of time. Shortly after arriving out here I contacted Bryan to ask whether he would be interested in selling early 19th Century engravings of Istanbul and its environs as I knew of a source for such things in the UK. Being in the Turkish section of the island, it seemed possible that there could be a flicker of interest. Bryan readily agreed and we built up some useful business together. To my chagrin, old maps and 19th century prints of Cyprus itself are virtually unobtainable as the relatively few produced have been much sought after by the Greek Cypriots for many decades and now fetch exorbitant prices – if they ever come on the market.

I should explain at this juncture how Bryan never had to advertise for staff – they just walked into the shop and ask for a job. Interestingly, from my point of view anyway, the usual applicants seemed to be beautiful young girls from various parts of the former Soviet Union, from Siberia to Georgia and often here to attend one of the many universities. Incredibly, they invariably spoke immaculate English and their understanding of the vernacular too meant that they could follow our schoolboy banter to an uncanny degree. At one stage however there was a lull in applicants and Bryan was a bit short-staffed so asked me if I'd help out, which I readily agreed to do. So he was forced for a while to shift from lovely young Russian girls to an ugly old Englishman, but happily for him this set-back did not last too long.

Bryan was also friendly with one of the local airline pilots, called Imri. He used to fly for Cyprus Turkish Airlines, but now operates for Emirates. He visited Bryan early one New Year to tell him about his New Year's Day experience. He was in Dubai, apparently, and was asked whether he would be prepared to fly an oil sheik who had hired one of their jets to take a party hawking on his estates somewhere in Arabia. As Imri's wife was in Cyprus and he had time on his hands, he was happy to agree.

When the aeroplane was opened for the sheik and his guests to embark, a flight of some fifty hooded hawks was brought in, each one carefully placed on its individual seat in Club Class accommodation. Their handlers and other members of the sheik's staff then processed into economy where they immediately lay down on the floor, while the sheik and his guests occupied First Class. When reporting in to air traffic for clearance, the tower asked whether all safety checks had been properly carried out. Imri was obliged to declare how the hawks could not be strapped in nor, under the odd circumstances, could the staff.

Once airborne, he said the hawks became excited at the sensation of flight and began flapping their wings in harmony with the aircraft. When asked over the radio for his destination airport, he had to say that he was bound for an un-named strip of concrete in the middle of nowhere. Wisely, air-traffic washed their hands of the flight from then on.

However, all went well, and at the end of the return flight, the sheik handed out envelopes to all crew members containing $5,000 for each and thanking them for a successful and truly enjoyable excursion. Imri was well-pleased as in addition to this, the sheik was due to pay $250,000 for the hire of the aircraft for the day. Oh, to own an oilfield somewhere…

On the subject of birds, I have a favourite one in Kyrenia, possibly a mynah bird. It, for I don't know whether it's male or female, lives in one of the main petrol station and repair garages and has built up an amazing variety

156

of calls. There is one guaranteed to put the fear of God into anyone unfamiliar with its performance. A pedestrian newcomer, risking a short cut across the forecourt, is likely to hear the loud and terrifying screech of braking tyres immediately behind him. The effect is devastating as the unfortunate target, heart pounding, leaps for safety, puzzling later over the mysterious disappearance of the vehicle.

CHAPTER XI

BUYING THE LAND

After two years in our rented villa, Meryl and I felt confident enough to settle in North Cyprus and to think about building our own home. As noted before, we had found it of immense value to experiment with living here and to find out about the disadvantages as well as the obvious pluses.

Naturally, the first thing was to discover a suitable plot. At that time, in 2001, land was not only plentiful but relatively cheap. There are pitfalls however, not recognised so well at that time but there nevertheless. After the Turkish intervention of 1974, the two populations were moved into their appropriate sectors, north or south of the Great Divide. The Greek propaganda machine is clever at concentrating on their removal from the north under protest but conveniently forgets how the Turkish Cypriots too were driven from their homes in the south. A great number of them lived in and around Paphos, Limassol and Larnaca, as well as in the capital Nicosia, and owned collectively vast tracts of land in these places.

Many of those displaced from their southern properties were offered former Greek land on what was termed the 'points system'. Put simply, although the exact calculations were complicated, the amount of land they were awarded depended on their title deeds showing how much they had owned in the south. Not all former Greek land was thus awarded and, over time, this residue became known as TRNC land, the Turkish Republic of North Cyprus. The trap was, and is still to some extent, that the unwary buyer would be lured into paying for land or property that did not have a clear and clean title deed. As this book is being prepared, an action is being brought by Greek Cypriots against a British family that purchased 'their' land in Lapta (Lapithos) and renovated the house on it. Naturally, this is a classic test case and, should it be upheld, thousands more prosecutions will no doubt enter the lists.

The Greeks have felt able to do this following the admission into the EU in May 2004 of the 'Republic of Cyprus', which includes the geographical whole of the island. Brussels apparently believed they were acting in good faith, in that the Greek Cypriots had a gentlemen's agreement with them to reach a settlement with the North through the proposals put forward in the UN plan, produced by its Secretary General, Kofi Annan, before admission to the bloc and following referenda that took place in both parts of the island. However, once the die was cast, the 'wily Greeks' campaigned vigorously on their side for a 'No' vote, with the Orthodox church telling its believers they would never reach Heaven if they voted for the plan. Consequently, 75% of Greek Cypriots condemned the plan and wasted months of hard work by Kofi Annan and his team, while the Turkish Cypriots voted for it with 65% in favour.

Safely ensconced now in the EU, the Greeks feel emboldened to seek help from the British courts in recovering 'their' lands. Should the British owners of the villa in question in Lapta default on any payment or compensation awarded, the Greeks ask for their property in the UK to be ordered sold and the money handed over. Not surprisingly, the uncertainty this tactic created has slowed the property boom current in the north throughout 2003, 2004 and 2005.

Certainly, one solid benefit to come out of the long and tedious negotiations has been the softening of the border between north and south. Initiated originally by the North, only Cypriot citizens initially were allowed to pass freely across the divide. At first it was through the original Ledra Palace crossing only, but as the scheme developed this was made into a pedestrian crossing exclusively, with another road built to the west of the city to permit motor traffic. As with Berlin, one can see the border becoming more porous almost daily. The UN is gradually clearing the thousands of mines sown within the border strip by both sides and more crossings are opening gradually along the whole of its length. It is of enormous benefit for both sides to get across and see the other part of this small island. There is nothing finer than people-contact to foster good relationships instead of allowing the politicians to dictate terms and condtions. Again, as with Berlin, it will be impossible now to close the border again. True, there are some unpleasant confrontations with a certain element from the south, still burning with resentment over the Turkish 'invasion' as they see it and the subsequent 'plundering' of their land and property. Happily, though, such sentiments are rare and the young especially seem to be free of resentment towards each other.

At the outset of these arrangements, and having announced how only Turkish Cypriots would be allowed in, all ex-pats living in the north were told they would be arrested on attempting to cross to the south, but to their lasting credit the EU said they would not permit any such thing as they do not recognise borders within member states so here we are, allowed to 'pass without let or hindrance' as required in our passports. The ladies really enjoy this unexpected access to the wider range of shops in the south with Marks and Spencer and Debenhams in Nicosia and a further two branches of M&S in other southern towns. There is a large DIY branch of Kingfisher UK to the south of Nicosia, to keep the menfolk happy too, and this also proves a useful addition to what we can now get on the island. Best of all perhaps, is the enormously wide variety of food and other commodities available in the large supermarkets, and it is useful to be able to buy things still unavailable in the North, a wide variety of European cheeses in particular.

Aware early on that problems existed with land purchase, Meryl and I were anxious to buy something with clean deeds and with the help of a sympathetic estate agent we have known for many years, we located and bought a one-and-a-half donum plot outside the village of Ozanköy, from an Englishman who had owned it since February 1974, significantly before the intervention which took place in July of that year. A gently sloping site, lying against the curve of a deep ravine, it enjoyed

161

distant views of the sea, through mature pine trees and over olive groves, about two miles to the north. To the south, about a mile away rose the graceful mountain chain, its rock faces gleaming white in the sun and the bosky greenery dabbed here and there in variegated shades. We could just glimpse a part of Bellapais abbey high above, also white but bathed in golden flood-light after sunset so that it seemed to float among the shadows of the hills. All in all, a magical spot and, the deal done, we couldn't wait to start building.

Building the house

We made enquiries about builders and were guided to Ali, a man with a fine reputation for excellent workmanship and straight dealing. I stress the latter point because many builders happily quote a price, reasonable in the extreme, and all is agreed. The system in force here is that a substantial deposit is put down with the chosen builder before he will begin work. Sometimes, after a fair start, the client is approached and told that some unforeseen problem has arisen and more money will be required before the project can continue. In the UK, we might argue that the builder should have taken greater care over his estimate, and extra costs outside his original quote are up to him. Quite so; but the builder here is always ahead of the game financially and rather than argue outside his mother tongue he simply fails to turn up. He assumes, genuinely perhaps, that the client is thinking things over and will eventually come to see and understand the builder's dilemma. In other words, you must agree to pay up before he will proceed further.

Sadly, this is likely to occur on more than one occasion, so that in the end the house costs far more than planned. *Caveat emptor!* Buyer beware.

Meryl and I took to Ali immediately with his warm friendly smile, quietly spoken voice and honest green eyes. On explaining our mission, he took us to meet his architect partner, Mehmet. Mehmet too was a genuine character and, having spent some time in the UK under training, spoke excellent English and was used to dealing with the resident Brits.

Over the next few weeks, we put together our modest bungalow and once the essential requirements were agreed the drawings were produced. Although I had always been interested in architecture and buildings in general, my first love was for cathedrals and medieval churches. Bungalows were something new but much less ambitious. Nevertheless, I was intrigued by the different construction techniques required for Cyprus. Typically, Cypriot buildings seem always to contain little steps – up and down. It is to accommodate differing levels of the land, of course, but it seems so easy to me to maintain one level throughout a simple bungalow and avoid the irritation of tripping or falling. Mehmet humoured me.

First, it was borne in on me that we live in an earthquake zone. Severe 'quakes in 2001 and 2002 in Turkey and Greece respectively helped drive the point home and I was anxious to see that we would be as well protected as possible. With everything agreed and all in place to allow us to proceed by February 2002, work began accordingly. The first problem we found was fitting the building to the site. We had provided Mehmet with a copy of the government site plan for our area of the village of Ozanköy. It may seem difficult to believe but I understand the last comprehensive Ordnance Survey, upon which the country's detailed land area maps are still based, was carried out by no less a person than Lord Kitchener in 1881, at that time a humble lieutenant and outside the peerage. Incidentally, for those interested in his original survey map, it is housed in sections in the Official Archives in Kyrenia. When assembled it is about 20ft long. Over a period of 120-odd years more than a few topographical changes have taken place and, not to put too fine a point on it, much of our land surface had seemingly slipped into the deep ravine that ran alongside our plot. Therefore, to some extent, Mehmet was trying to build out in space although, of course, our original boundaries were still there to be located somewhere in the depths below.

Eventually, the house was marked out again, its far corner very near to the cliff edge and the JCB digger moved in. The first step was to set up a grid with posts and twine and mark out the positions of the foundation pillars with white plaster powder. Next, deep holes were excavated, a metre square and another deep. Into these were set cages made on site out of steel reinforcing rods, some 2 cms in diameter. These are delivered to the site folded half way along their length of 10 metres or so to fit on the flat-bed lorry that delivers them, and cut to size as required by a special steel guillotine device that takes a lot of muscle to operate. As with much of the building work out here, it is very labour intensive and the workers usually have to toil in all weathers, the most cruel being the pitiless summer sun. Invariably, there is little or no shade on a site so the visible parts of their bodies are burned black. Surprisingly, one very rarely sees a building worker without a long-sleeved shirt and long trousers, regardless of the temperature which can reach 50 degrees Celsius on some days in high summer.

More iron rods, longer and of a thinner gauge now, were tied together with wire and laid horizontally in trenches to link each cubed hole. Locked into the tops of the ground cages were more rods, vertical this time and also tied with wire to keep them in place. These would form the centres for the upright stanchions that were to frame the house. Once in place, wooden planks were nailed side by side and set around all the ironwork – shuttering – to contain the poured concrete. As the building progressed, more concrete beams formed a ring uniting the tops of the uprights and others crossed over from front to back. Eventually, the steel-reinforced ceiling was cast on more wooden planks held in place by dozens of makeshift supports fashioned out of discarded shuttering left over from previous builds. I used to think the finished structure at that stage looked like something Costain's might have erected to carry a B-road over the M6. Once, I counted the number of upright stanchions and found the total came to 36. Oh dear: I began to pray that our ugly grey duckling would eventually be turned into a beautiful white swan.

Mehmet was amused at my concerns and explained how the destructive power of an earthquake gets to work, shaking and twisting the building as well as punching up from beneath if the force is severe enough and close by.

Why on earth did we begin this foolhardy escapade? It was for this reason we had to agree the reinforced concrete ceiling over the roof area to complete the building's structural integrity, whereas I was keen on plaster-board and pitched timber above to improve insulation. I knew from experience how houses with solid concrete flat roofs cost a fortune to heat in winter and another to cool in the summer months. However, Mehmet did concede the pitched timber roof, hipped and gabled, set out on the ceiling and topped off with with re-cycled clay roof tiles. That part at least looked pretty and earned Meryl's approval. Looked at individually, the tiles vary in their colours depending on where they were placed in the kiln. Creams, reds, ochres, oranges and yellows can be discerned, while the deeper shades hint at delicate suggestions of green and blue. Shuffled randomly during the cleaning process, the tiles are fixed on battens nailed on top of the roof's insulation material, giving a glorious overall warm finish to the roof, like a subtly-coloured cosy over a teapot.

In our discussions with Mehmet, I had laboured my belief in damp-proof membranes for floors and walls, and insulation to a point where I suspect boredom had set in. One day, though, he showed me a new type of building block that was relatively new to the island and called 'Y-tong' – pronounced 'Yew-tong' by the locals. Manufactured in Turkey, it is light-weight, resistant to damp, and thermally efficient but solid enough to contribute to sound reduction. Although not load-bearing, this did not matter as the blocks were used merely to fill in as panels between the steel-reinforced concrete framework. Huzza! We quickly settled for them. Combined with the other materials we'd selected to reduce damp and increase insulation, it proved an excellent choice. Discovering how double-glazing was by that time readily available on the island, we opted for that too as part of the strategy.

The shell of the villa completed, it was time to move on to the 'finishing'. This included plastering or rendering the walls with a mixture of sand and cement, agreeing the lighting and power points, plumbing for the loos, baths and showers and radiator positions which were then all marked out on walls or floors with a red aerosol spray. Amusing to me was how at one stage in all this I was invited to assist in the placing of the lavatory bowls. As the waste pipes were already positioned in the concrete flooring it was a matter of agreeing which was the best way to face when seated. After much debate and experimenting when everyone joined in, the exact placing of the loos was agreed to general acclaim and satisfaction.

I should at this point pay the credit due Ali's men. Most were from Turkey's despised Kurdish community, over on the island to find work enough to send money back to their families at home across the sea. At first, they presented a terrifying sight: slim and very fit from years of gruelling physical work, wild hair, dark skinned and with naturally ferocious expressions – they are after all renowned for their fighting skills and tenacity in battle – so we kept a cautious distance. The Kurds had proved great allies in the struggle to overcome Saddam Hussein's reign of terror, as they had plenty of old scores to settle with the tyrant and his henchmen. Our builders were very proud of the part they played in Saddam's defeat. The Turks, on the other hand, seem ill at ease with their Kurdish compatriots and nurse a perpetual fear of their demands for an independent Kurdish homeland in eastern Turkey. With the local Cypriots, as well as with us, there was also a language problem, since Kurds have their own tongue, quite different from Turkish. Adding to their tough appearance, it seemed that the concept of shaving regularly was quite alien to them; after all, who needs to look smart when working and sleeping on a building site for six days a week, sometimes seven?

After a time, however, we established a rewarding rapport with these extremely skilled workers and came to hold them in great respect. As a bonus for me, I discovered they have a well-developed and mischievous sense of humour. There was one time when Meryl accompanied me to see for herself the progress being made. I would go down daily but she preferred to make occasional forays only, as the concrete skeleton and what the place would look like when finished were all a mystery to her. When we arrived, the brothers Hüseyin and Ramadan (the latter known affectionately by his co-workers as Rambo) were working on the plastering of a series of arches that formed the outer wall of what I called the cloister at the rear of the house. Meryl was horrified to see them using lengths of different-coloured string, knotted in several places to mark their straight line along the wall, twigs broken from a nearby shrub and stuck in the cement to hold each end. I drew attention to this which they thought a huge joke and laughed uproariously. Meryl need not have worried. I looked along the section when it was finished and found it in perfect plane and plumb throughout its entire length and height.

String, or twine, seemed to play an important part in house building. It was also used on the ground to mark out areas where something was to be constructed. Mehmet, for some reason beyond my understanding, always preferred green twine, a very effective camouflage against the foliage. To the unwary which included me, it was easy to miss seeing the twine altogether and trip headlong into the thorny scrub that grows close to the ground everywhere. The builders got used to my anguished yells and ignored them as I regularly fell into these traps but I suspect they secretly chuckled as they listened to my fluent curses.

Hüseyin was a most amusing and entertaining character because in view of the language difficulty, with Turkish as well as with English as noted above, he had become a superb mime artist; Marcel Marceau could have learned from him, I feel sure. I called at the site one afternoon to find Hussein laying tiles to form a path alongside the house to the rear garden. It looked rather on the narrow side to me and the window sills for the study and the sitting room protruded into the line of the path at chest height. I conveyed this worry to Hussein who stood up, checked the width and limits of the path in the manner of a Hollywood film director, walked back up to the top and squinted along the track he had marked out. He signalled to me to take note and set off, making exaggerated, swerving motions to prevent his shoulders colliding with the sills. Performance over, he grinned with satisfaction and returned to work. I, on the other hand, was reminded of a North Sea fisherman struggling along the deck of a Grimsby trawler in a Force 8 gale.

On another occasion I spotted him early one morning waiting in Ozanköy's small village square next to the mosque. As I was driving into Girne, I stopped and offered him a lift. His face clouded over and he looked startled. I was puzzled at first, but he began to indicate how he was waiting to be collected by his co-workers. Were he to accept my offer, they would arrive in the truck; he would be gone! Consternation would overtake everyone, panic would set in. Heads would be scratched, eyes shaded from the sun as a thorough scanning of the area would be conducted by all. I could imagine too messengers sent hither and yon, to seek for news of Hussein's mysterious disappearance and it seemed there would soon be the rending of garments and gnashing of teeth. I motioned that I would travel on alone and was rewarded with a beaming smile and a cheery wave.

My favourite mime of Hussein's, though, was that of the wicked serpent. Going to the villa one morning, I was horrified to see the body of a yellow snake lying on the garden wall. I went to remonstrate with Hussein who held up an imperious hand to silence any protest and set about portraying for me what had happened. One of the men was looking for something. As he searched, the snake emerged suddenly from the undergrowth right by his feet. Hussein skipped backwards with the agility of a mountain goat, his face rigid with fear. Unless the snake was killed, it could attack one of them and it was of the venomous variety. First, there would be the surprise of the sudden bite, followed by the shock of realising what had happened. Hussein's eyelids began to flutter, the facial muscles went into spasm. As his limbs twitched, a great deal of dramatic staggering followed as the poison took effect. Eventually, he

170

seemed to become less agitated and the jerky movements lessened. Gradually, his eyes rolled back into their sockets, the lids closed and a look of ineffable calm suffused his features as one witnessed the soul leaving the body and departing on its journey to join Allah. As a spiritual gesture of his submission to fate, Hussein's arms crossed over on his chest in a final act of piety. A truly fabulous performance, and a complete joy to watch.

As the months passed, the house continued to take shape with plumbers and electricians following each other in sequence as they completed the various stages of their installations. Another decision, after much discussion, was the inclusion of a central heating system operated by LPG, also recently available in the North. The only supplier of the fuel at that time came to inspect the site and to confirm whether or not he would risk his heavy supply lorry to bounce along our very rough track, called euphemistically a 'stone road', as it was quite a heavy vehicle and represented a major investment. He was not at all willing initially and it was only by the persuasive powers of Ali and Mehmet together and, I suspect, the odd threat, that he reluctantly agreed. Shortly afterwards, a substantial, white cylindrical gas tank arrived, about two metres long and a metre in diameter that had to be unloaded by a JCB acting as crane and carefully placed alongside the bungalow, near enough to allow straightforward connections to the combi-boiler; thus called as it heats the household water in the winter as well as the radiators. A little more cheerful on this occasion, the gas man produced a fat invoice for the down-payment/deposit for the gas tank.

The gas itself arrives as a result of a telephone call to the depot in Lefkoşa. The first question we're asked is about the condition of our rough track, always a difficult one to answer honestly. As we need further gas supplies in the wet winter months, obviously, the surface is often appalling; muddy, slippery and very tricky to negotiate as would be the Police Driving School's skid-pan at Henley. I try to be as vague as possible implying that there's really nothing that a skilled driver couldn't handle. Understandably, perhaps, the firm's owner Mustafa, is rather precious about his lorries, with their low-slung under-carriages and highly dangerous loads. When the truck eventually makes it to our bungalow, its arrival is dramatic and impressive. Painted fire-engine red with white lettering and warning signs, it sports crimson flags streaming at each corner and I often think it would not look out of place processing through Red Square in Moscow on May 1st. Once in position, however, the driver uncouples an important-looking armoured hose and drags it across to our tank. He then produces a huge bunch of keys and flicks through them until he finds the one that unlocks our feed valve. The hose is coupled up, the dials on the lorry set at zero – I am always obliged to witness this – and the filling proceeds. After some 1000 litres or so are pumped in, the hose is wound back on to the truck and the driver produces a large calculator to work out the cost. After a series of complicated sums I am presented with another eye-watering bill and ask nervously whether they will accept an English cheque drawn in sterling, and they happily do. And, after some three winters of enjoying full central heating, Meryl and I agree it was a sound and worthwhile investment.

After more careful thought, Meryl and I decided we would have a swimming pool, despite the chronic problem with water on the island. Having had to discard Plan A, which was to build the pool in the 'L' of the house shape against the side of the ravine and finding that the land had gone, we proceeded to Plan B and set it in the back garden, still against the ravine side as it curved round the edge of the plot. As building of the pool progressed, Mehmet asked if we wanted a design in the tiling on the bottom and after some discussion we opted for his company's logo, derived from his family name Üçok, with the Üç meaning three and ok, arrows. Hence, the design consisted of a central straight arrow, with one either side curving outwards, rather like a trident. The arrow shafts sat on a series of lines that got shorter as they tiered down. Mehmet was flattered and took it as a compliment to his design for our villa, which indeed it was. However, I couldn't resist teasing him and told him the real reason was that should the pool end up in the ravine, being very near to the edge, everyone would know who was the architect responsible. (PLATE 14)

When the time came to insure the house a young English lady we know who deals with such things came to look round. We discussed the building, its fittings and contents and were almost finished when she asked about the pool. I found this quite entertaining and asked how it could be taken away on a lorry or catch fire. 'Earthquakes, Adrian?' she enquired. We insured the pool.

There proved to be many more compensations with the pool than we could have imagined. Despite being unable to position it where we originally planned, it is still in a sheltered position and not, so far, overlooked. After a time, I realised it was ridiculous to keep changing wet trunks for dry for up to five times a day in the hot weather when there was no one else about, so from then on, I bathed *au naturel* when dipping and frolicking in the cool waters. Meryl refused either to frolic or to dip *au naturel* - something to do with overhead spy satellites I think.

Water, or the lack of it, is a constant cause for concern of course. As more and more houses rise from the ruins of the olive and citrus groves and the almond orchards, most are constructed with swimming pools in their gardens, thus exacerbating the already acute shortage of water on the island.

It is fascinating though to watch the incredible variety of wild life that sees our pool apparently as one of the area's favourite watering holes. I have always suspected that the deep ravine alongside is a natural haven for all manner of insects, butterflies, birds, small reptiles and even snakes. The pool is an 'overflow' type, meaning that the water overlaps the gently-sloping edge and spills into a surrounding gully before returning to what is termed a 'balance' tank whence it is pumped back into the pool. This happy arrangement means that each creature can find its ideal depth as it approaches the edge of the water. So, at the lower end of the scale we have the 'resident' insects, led by tiny wood-boring wasps that creep timidly to the edge of the water to sip. Once they've had their fill, I watch them fly back into our timbered roof and continue their life's work of devouring it.

Their big brothers are the bees and proper wasps, followed by very large four-engine hornets. One keeps a respectful distance from these latter chaps as they possess a very powerful sting indeed, but fortunately they are not aggressive and don't buzz around one irritatingly like the British Standard wasp. Our burgeoning garden attracts several varieties of butterfly as we hoped it would, many gorgeously attired in their fine liveries, and they too like to drink at the pool. Then there are the birds with their lovely antics. From small sparrows, great tits, robins, the black and white Cyprus warbler, to magpies and large black and grey crows, they gather to drink and to bathe and seem greatly to enjoy their elaborate cleaning and preening routines afterwards. Cooing wood pigeons enter the water chest-first, soaking their breast feathers and then, after a brisk shake, actually push out into the pool a little way despite not having webbed feet. The swallows and house martins too are a delight with their displays of brilliant aerobatics as they scoop up water in their beaks to make mud for their nests or to give to their young. Meryl quite rightly bemoans the amount of water our visitors consume one way or another, especially as we're paying around £100 per month for it in the summer. After dusk, the night-shift takes over with frogs first, emerging from goodness-knows-where to croak away in the shallows. If I approach, they dive in and swim around elegantly like Jeremy Fisher until I go away again. Then it is the turn of the bats and owls to dip in and help themselves as they manoeuvre skilfully overhead. I love watching, as much as one can, in starlight. With owls' wings tipped by special feathers to eliminate the sound of their approach to their prey - and bats are pretty streamlined too - sometimes one hears only the 'plop' as they dip their beaks in while skimming silently over at incredible speeds. A gentle surge of rings follows afterwards, spreading softly to the pool's edges and wrinkling the reflection of the spangled sky.

Birds were by no means interesting in the pool alone. In the autumn months of September and October one would be sitting quietly in the garden and be puzzled at strange and unusual noises. At last realising they were coming from overhead, one would look up to see dozens, sometimes hundreds of migrating birds flying over. Most seemed to be of the stork or heron families, squawking to each other as they flew in ragged formations towards the east. Often, they would over-circle a large area, apparently seeking somewhere suitable to land, find food and rest for the night. It seems that most migrating birds aim ultimately for the Rift Valley that runs south through Israel, Jordan and into northeast Africa, and thought to have been a key navigating landmark for birds over millions of years, while Cyprus is the ideal stopping off zone while en route from the north or west. Many visiting tourists as well as locals come or wait for these wonderful sights and arrive equipped with field glasses and sophisticated cameras to witness and capture these annual dramas of Nature. Sometimes, at the coastal areas, one can spot flocks of smaller birds assembling over the sea to fly off for the winter. Being small they create less noise, and so remain almost invisible unless one is prepared for their departure and knows where to lie in wait...

Eventually, the house was finished, with the electricity connected following long and tedious negotiations with the authorities, at the end of which I had to fling them a large purse of gold, much to my great chagrin. Well, Ali said we needed eight wooden poles to reach our house from the nearest supply point and one paid so-much per pole. Sometime afterwards, I walked down the line checking but, even after three goes at it, could count only seven. I pointed out this deficiency to Ali, who grinned and drew my attention to an eighth pole installed as a stout prop for one of the seven. This was used to brace it against the tug of the cables as they were bent forward to follow the line of the lane. To this day, I still wonder whether that rather low, fast one was really fair.

Having felt a little ripped off with the electricity, we decided against spending another fortune bringing piped water to the bungalow. We could after all, rely on water brought by tankers, several tonnes at a time, so that is what we did. Connecting into the telecommunications system posed similar problems, so we use mobile 'phones only and brilliant they are too. My precious computer is used as just a word processor which, quite frankly, is about the limit of my computer skills anyway. It was presented at my retirement bash with 'The Complete Idiot's Guide to the Internet' for good reason and I hope one day I shall need to explore its contents.

Ali was to prove a good and generous friend. Knowing that we would have to do without electricity for the first week or two until Kibtek, the North's authority in these matters, would be available to check everything and agree to connect us to the supply, he gave us a brand-new 4kw generator as a most welcome house-warming present. Also, knowing how his cabinet-maker chum was so good at carpentry, we had asked if he would make for us a matching pair of bathroom cabinets. Meryl had seen a photograph in a magazine showing a pretty, delicate antique piece she greatly liked, that seemed to be made from thin pine wood and this she gave to Ali as a pattern. Early one morning some time later I watched as our site foreman, Mustafa, stopped his truck outside. As he came down the drive, I noticed he was obviously carrying something very heavy so I rushed to open the front door for him. He almost fell into the hall and quickly set down the first of the cabinets, breathing heavily, and returned to fetch its partner. I went to pick up the first one and discovered that it was knees together and back straight or another session at the physiotherapist loomed. Beautifully made, the joiner had used MDF painted white which meant they were considerably thicker and heavier than pine. But, so robustly were they crafted that one could have safely put to sea in either of them. As it was, I had to have heavy-gauge galvanised corner brackets specially made in order to fix them to the bathrooms' walls. However, once done and put in place, they look splendid and Meryl was delighted. Typically, dear Ali would not accept a penny piece.

CHAPTER XII
TAKING POSSESSION

All inadequacies apart, we moved in at the end of November 2002, Ali's men helping us to the end with moving our effects from the rented house, by road three miles away. Meryl and I brought the cats down and at first they seemed to settle in their unfamiliar, new surroundings. After three days, however, Panda disappeared. Toffee never budged, her natural intelligence accepting that home was where we were. Having searched fruitlessly for many hours, we decided against real hope that he might have returned to the old house, although we could hardly believe Panda would find his way. Sure enough, there he was, so we gently brought him back with a quiet but stern lecture. Panda returned a further three times but by now the winter rains had set in. After travelling across to the deserted house, to find it darkened and locked up, the cold rain battering down with relentless fury, poor Panda presented a pathetic sight, soaked through his soft white fur, bewildered, hungry and miserable. We just could not understand his reluctance to stay with us; safe, well-fed, warm and dry. The fifth attempt at escape almost ended in tragedy, as he actually returned to the bungalow after being missing for several hours again. Once more he was soaking and dishevelled but this time he was also injured to the extent he could hardly drag himself along with his front legs. His earlier trips must have taken him two miles across country, but he had also to negotiate two busy roads in order to reach the house. Even now we do not know, nor ever will, what exactly happened to him, but the story has a happy ending. Our super new vet, Pertev, following Dr Türker's retirement, is a kind and caring young man and he took Panda away to nurse him back to health and did so most successfully. Realising that we would probably have the same problem again should Panda be brought back to the bungalow, Pertev managed to find him a new home in Lefkoşa, with a family that included two children who really loved and cossetted him and he settled in well, apparently. Meryl and I, although so sorry to see him go, were relieved and pleased to think he might be happy again.

Toffee's solitary reign did not last long. Several cats passed through the garden from time to time, but most were feral and we kept a cautious distance. One, a lean and mean black and white male job, took chunks of flesh out of my friendly, out-stretched hand, teaching me a valuable lesson. In time a black female with becoming, long fur and the single distinguishing feature of huge almond-shaped green eyes performed the usual pantomime and was allowed to stay. With great originality, we called her Ebony.

After settling in very quickly, Ebony began to play us up a good deal. Her nocturnal practice was to quit the home as Meryl and I were going to bed. Later, standing on her hind legs, she would pummel vigorously on our bedroom window with her front paws demanding admission, her favoured time being between two and four a.m. when we're at our best. Usually it was I who would awake first and stagger across the room to let her in. She would leap on to our bed between us and immediately embark on a thorough brush up and cleaning procedure. This produced a slightly nauseating motion, as though the bed had been pushed out to sea. The slurping noises as she got to the difficult bits added to the illusion. Once the larger chunks had been tugged from the tangle, they were spat out and broadcast over the bed, many of them perilously close to my ear. Add the odd tick released by the process that would start wandering along Meryl's shoulder, and you have the conditions for a lengthy bout of insomnia. I often gave up the idea of further sleep and opted for a strong brew of tea to restore the throbbing tissues, regardless of the hour. Equally often, I would forget to move cautiously in the dark with bare feet and tread on one of those burrs, also a by-product of the cleaning operation, upon which village blacksmiths modelled things for bringing down a French cavalry charge. None of this improves one's composure much and we wondered for a long time how to eradicate the problem without eradicating the cat. On another occasion, I awoke in the night with a strange and unpleasant feeling in my mouth – a gamey taste and slightly gritty, only to discover that one of Ebony's back paws was in it. Fortunately a large bottle of Listerine was handy in the bathroom; vigorous gargling probably saved me from all manner of ills and I have since learned to sleep with my mouth firmly shut when she is present.

Within a very short time, Meryl turned her attention to the garden, determined to convert it from building site to a lesser Eden. Various professionals stopped by to look and to offer advice and over a few months, things began slowly to take shape. First, the soil had to be cleaned of debris, broken up and sieved. Then, enriched topsoil and manure were brought in and mixed with what was already there. We wanted greenery at the front to shield us from the road and to filter out a lot of the dust from passing traffic as well as to protect us from feeling we were living in a goldfish bowl. First to arrive was a selection of young trees from a nursery and they were duly planted in a line alongside the boundary wall; a blue jacaranda, a white orchid tree, a pink almond, a yellow bignonia and a Judas tree. This latter one produces a lovely bright mauve blossom in the spring and is said to be the tree from which a bitterly remorseful Judas hanged himself after betraying Jesus in the Garden of Gethsemane for thirty pieces of silver.

The only significant survivor from the original vegetation on our plot was a much-valued, mature olive tree and we were determined it would not be sacrificed to our bungalow or pool. Happily it sits now in the perfect spot almost in the middle of the garden and with its superior height and girth has become its focal point. As the garden developed, Meryl could see more opportunities for new plants, shrubs and trees. As I was presented with all the bills for these additions I took a keen interest in the comings and goings. Sometimes, as an overloaded truck groaned down the driveway, green banners of lofty branches blowing in its slipstream, I was reminded of Macbeth's great fear as predicted by the Apparition, that of 'Birnam Wood coming to Dunsinane…'

Now, some three years on, the garden looks wonderful and is much admired by our friends and relations. I feel I can make this claim as the credit is entirely Meryl's and my part has been paymaster only.

One of the pleasanter sights from the house occasionally is the appearance of the local goatherd with his assorted flock of sheep and goats as he brings them up from the village to graze the area around us. It all looks very timeless, biblical even, but with the horrific building boom going on in the district there is progressively less and less pasture for them to nibble. On such occasions, we have to be on our guard and make sure the gates at the bottom of our drive are firmly shut. Goats seem to be permanently ravenous and will devour anything green with mesmerising speed and thoroughness, rather like four-footed locusts. To them, our garden must look like a goat's gourmet paradise.

The goatherd is a most agreeable chap and is always offering to sell us manure and hellim (goats' cheese). He is called Ahmed and usually accompanied by his lovely, dappled-grey dog that in theory herds the flock but seems pretty useless in that respect. In fact, many of the ancient shepherding customs are still practised here. In biblical times, the shepherd actually led his sheep or goats knowing each one individually and they would follow him anywhere. He would talk or call to them in a sort of strange 'chirruping', an incomprehensible 'language', said to be handed down from father to son and thought to have its origins in Aramaic, Jesus' own tongue. Jesus made much of shepherds, sheep and goats in His parables and we're not far from the Holy Land. In his book, *In the Steps of the Master*, the travel writer HV Morton records how in Palestine in the 1920s, he watched as two shepherds were chatting together in the early morning. They had spent the night at a small inn, their assorted flocks of sheep and goats thoroughly intermingled in the adjacent field. As the men went to move off on their different ways, each began calling to his animals to follow. Within a matter of minutes the two herds had separated completely and were contentedly following their respective masters. Certainly, Ahmed does 'talk' to his flock and tends to lead them himself, with the dog usually looking on in gormless admiration.

However, one morning during the summer, the dog suddenly turned up in our driveway on her own and refused to budge for some obscure reason. After a couple of hours, Meryl became concerned that she was lost or disorientated, and I was despatched to find Ahmed's old house in the village and to inform him of this unusual development. When I eventually found it in a quiet backwater it was late morning and, with no immediate sign of life, I knocked at the weather-beaten door. Bumps and rattles mixed with female chatter from within indicated that the family was indeed present but when the door opened there stood three women whom I guessed were Ahmed's wife and either daughters or daughters-in-law, all dressed in village garb of the Muslim tradition, together with several young children. Everyone emerged to stare at the foreigner in total silence, their expressions registering disbelief, as though I had miraculously descended from a nearby spaceship. Plainly the English language was something with which

184

their ears had never been troubled so it was difficult to explain my mission of mercy.

I managed to ascertain that the men-folk were occupied elsewhere. Then, by means of what I felt to be some rather ingenious miming, and borrowing freely from Hüseyin's repertoire, I tried to establish the presence of the lost dog, languishing in our drive. My stooping posture with elaborate hand gestures to indicate a dog's body, accompanied by woofing noises was decidedly a move in the wrong direction as it merely caused the younger women to gather the children closer into their skirts, all too obviously convinced I was not only dangerous but had provided clear proof that I was literally 'barking'. I could almost hear the police sirens.

Fortunately, a workman with a smattering of English was painting a house nearby and after a little valuable translation, the ladies grew calmer. Having withdrawn in some disarray, my nerve completely shattered, I was greatly relieved when the dog was recovered safely an hour later.

Two years on from the bungalow's completion in 2002 and inevitably the odd, minor problems began to arise. It was a Sunday morning in mid-November and Meryl, while I was away at church, had noticed how a small but steady trickle of water was coming off the roof outside the kitchen and reported it to me on my return. It had happened before and proved to be caused by a stuck ball-cock in the cold-water tank. The cylindrical tank itself was made of polypropylene, designed to hold a tonne, and was laid on its side like a barrel. The overflowing water is conducted across the concrete roof and finds its way down one of the gargoyles that take the rainwater off the cloister walk. In the past it had required only a quick blip to loosen up the chalk sediment and to impress Meryl with my plumbing prowess. Freeing the ladder from its stowage I manhandled it through the house and propped it beneath the small door high in the wall of the sunroom that gives access to the loft, the only room the full height of the building. On this occasion it seemed the lime-scale had finally won the contest as my initial inspection showed that the float was fully submerged beneath the water inlet and even the most frantic blipping elicited no favourable response.

I had insisted that the tanks were concealed in the roof space when the house was under construction as I think they look so ugly suspended on iron frames well above the roof line and silhouetted against the sky, which is normal practice. Also, it would have spoiled the natural appearance of the roofline with its old Roman tiles. I digress, I know, but whenever the word 'silhouette' is used, I am always reminded of an old chum who swore that his elderly aunt, suffering from a severe form of malapropism, always referred to slender fir trees as 'stiletto-ed' against the sky. To this day, I think the sheer poetry of the Italian far out-matches the French; a sharper and more vivid description than the slightly banal 'silhouette'.

When the plumber was installing the water systems, I had particularly asked for overflow pipes to be connected and extended to the outside of the roof and was assured, 'don't worry; no problem.' I should explain that this is the Turkish Cypriots' favourite response to awkward requests. At that juncture I ought to have recognised the danger but, with so many other things to get done, I did not. Sure enough, I found that on examining the position more carefully for the first time, I could see that no effective overflow pipes existed. So, I was urged reluctantly into the field by a worried wife, and the pressure was on. Unfortunately, we had agreed earlier to escort the new chaplain of St Andrew's, the Rev Tony Jeynes and his wife Irene, to luncheon after their first Sunday service so it was not until late afternoon, under a lowering sky precipitating the rapid onset of darkness, that I was able to begin assessing the problem. A 'modest' amount of drink had been taken which gave me a rather cocksure attitude toward the job in hand.

As the tank had been shoe-horned into the low-pitched roof space, its circular lid about 18 inches in diameter and lying alongside, having blown off in one of last winter's gales, and too near the timbers anyway to fit on properly, things did not look too promising. Working within the feeble light from a torch in the top of the tank with mole wrench and spanners proved more of a challenge to the dextrous skills than I had imagined. The alcohol-induced euphoria quickly evaporated.

The builders out here are still not fully conversant with professional construction techniques required of tiled wooden roofs, and my first discovery, made by scalp, was that several batten nails had missed their parent purlin or rafter and were protruding an inch or so into the roof space. Despite the intervening two years having welded together the metal parts I was trying to disengage, the roof nails had lost none of their pristine sharpness. Consequently, I administered a sort of DIY-trepanning operation on my skull each time I hitched myself higher in an attempt to get a better purchase on the more obdurate bits of copper and brass or to see more clearly what I was doing. I was dimly aware somewhere in my subconscious of Meryl calling up from time to time, '*Must* you use that sort of language on a Sunday?'.

The final straw broke when the split-pin I had so laboriously worked loose and tried to replace after cleaning everything slipped softly and irretrievably into the abyss and sank to the bottom of the tank. Another despairing cry from Meryl. At that late hour operations had to be suspended until a new ball-cock assembly could be purchased at crack of dawn the following morning. I had ruefully to admit to Meryl how I reckon I am getting too old to clamber up ladders and work in small spaces under poor light, and felt absolutely bushed for the next day or so.

As it was, full and frank discussions took place between Meryl and me about correct methods of holding ladders steady without killing the user. It is ridiculous really, as I surveyed torn fingernails, gouged hands and barked shins, not to mention bleeding through my hair, all from what should be the simplest of tasks. No wonder the gorgeous young ladies at our local supermarket insist on carrying out my heavier purchases and placing them

188

carefully in the car boot. Clearly, I am seen nowadays as a sheep in sheep's clothing and that's also pretty demoralising.

Fortunately, we have contact with a really super plumber who lives up the mountain in Bellapais. To my delight, he quickly turned disaster into triumph and fixed all with the help of his twelve-year-old son who, in the role of 'gofer', flew up and down the ladder like a swallow building its nest. More humiliation for me, but we now have proper over-flows on both the cold and hot tanks, so I'm hoping for no more puddles in the roof, with luck.

For some time before and after we moved in to the bungalow, Meryl and I wondered what we should call the place, as many friends used to ask where we lived. As the house is a long way from any recognisable landmark it was a fair question. We had it in mind to call it A&M, with most people we consulted thinking it stood for Adrian and Meryl, but in fact it was 'Ancient and Modern' and in the correct order so far as Meryl was concerned. I hankered after the old logo that used to be embossed on all Ancient and Modern Hymn books but have had a very difficult job tracking one down. In the meantime, as if to pre-empt this move and quickly snuff out any pretentious ideas, the Ozanköy Mukhtar pulled up outside in his truck one day with one of his henchmen and nailed up on the electricity pole immediately at the top of our drive a small blue and white metal plaque announcing prosaically 'H61'. I don't mind too much but Meryl points out that no one has ever yet found us armed only with this information. As I write, the debate goes on...

CHAPTER XIII

ST ANDREW'S CHURCH IN KYRENIA

I have already mentioned St Andrew's Church and its chaplain. Although I had been a regular church-goer in the UK for many years, and had served on parochial church councils, I had rather lost confidence in Christianity since my divorce in 1982. Meryl has been brought up in the Quaker tradition, which included schooldays boarding at Sibford near Banbury, in Oxfordshire, so regular church-going has never been part of her life. However, the discipline of silence imposed by her religion very quickly left Meryl once she quit her school and nowadays I seem to do most of the quaking.

On arriving and meeting the small ex-pat community in and around Kyrenia, it was not long before we came into contact with the friendly and Pickwickian figure of the Rev Anthony Fletcher, the resident chaplain of St Andrew's at that time, in 2002. Anthony was a former RAF chaplain and had seen service in Canada, Germany and the Falkland Islands as well as many other RAF outposts. His delightful wife, Jane, was an experienced practice nurse with a wealth of experience in dealing with the sick and the elderly both at home and abroad during her husband's postings. All of this was put to good use out here to the lasting benefit of many ex-pats in the wider Kyrenia area. During their 25 peripatetic years of marriage, they had managed to bring up their two boys, Matthew and Duncan, both of whom are developing useful and stimulating careers. Quite recently, and much to the family's delight, Matthew was called to the Bar in Lincoln's Inn.

Returning to my introduction at the beginning of this chapter, I did not feel quite ready to attend church. But without my knowledge or agreement, Meryl had some long private conversations with Anthony and told him of my past involvement with the Church in the UK, my former memberships of village PCCs, and her belief that I really wanted to return to worship. A short time later he invited me to come to the services and later again I was asked to join the Church Council, both of which I did.

I greatly enjoyed attending each Sunday after so many years away, and to share the warm friendship of St Andrew's congregation and fellow council members. After even more time, I was asked to serve as Chaplain's warden and accepted happily, despite having the strong conviction I was the fourth person he'd asked. The Fletchers left in 2004, having worked hard to initiate and complete the restoration and refurbishment of the church.

During Anthony's time here, several fund-raising events were organised and usually one of them each year was the Harvest Supper held at a suitable restaurant in early October. But, one year it was decided to introduce a 4th of July fancy dress competition with Anthony as judge. The evening was great fun and went with a particularly good swing; delicious food, copious volumes of excellent wines and lively music. The time came for Anthony, elevated on a couple of beer crates, to deliver his verdict on the costumes. Standing on her own just in front of him was a very popular member of the congregation, and famous island-wide for her magnificent *embonpoint*. She was wearing a white angora sweater that evening embroidered with small sequins and other glittery things. For some reason there was a spotlight shining down on her that made the jumper twinkle in the most beguiling manner. Announcing the winner over the microphone, Anthony said, 'and for the best breasts – I mean the best dressed…' I can only think Anthony must have become somewhat distracted by the lady but he ever after refused to say whether it was an accident or deliberate mistake. As I said to Harry sitting next to me, had there been such a competition, she surely would have won hands down, if one could use that expression.

Many years after our first meeting, Anthony confided in me how, on being invited to a black-tie dinner, he had always wished for a clergyman's dress outfit which seems to be modelled on the clothes they wore in the 18th Century. All of it in black, except for the deep clerical collar, it apparently consists of a broad-brimmed hat that fits the crown closely, the usual fly-buttoned shirt with full dog-collar, cut-away tail-coat, knee-breeches with silk hose, and silver-buckled shoes. I have never met another Clerk in Holy Orders better suited in my opinion to such an outfit and remain disappointed at never having seen Anthony thus accoutred.

Established in 1913, St Andrew's church building has been the focal point for Anglican worship in the area for almost a century. It is believed to have started off as a simple room on the present site, the land having been donated by Mr. George Houstoun, a member of an old Colonial family. Another, the Macdonalds, funded the building and dedicated the gift as a memorial to their son who died as a teenager while at Malvern College in 1918. The years passed, and the congregation expanded as many British people came to the area either to retire or to work as part of the British Colonial community sent out to help administer the island. From records, we know that the church was extended at some time to include a chancel and modest transepts. In 1976, however, it became apparent that the chancel was beginning to separate from the nave as the chancel's foundations started to subside. Despite emergency remedial work to halt the slide, it had eventually to be demolished. Without adequate funds to rebuild it the unfortunate worshippers had to make do with the nave only. Blocking off the east end with a blank curtain wall relieved only by a simple, narrow cross cut in the stonework and glazed, the altar, communion rails and the rest of the church furniture had to be squeezed in. This left seating for only 70 worshippers, quite inadequate for the numbers wishing to attend the services.

So, the task facing the Chaplain and the church council in the early part of the 21st Century was a daunting one. Over earlier years, various schemes had been put forward to increase the seating, but none came to anything. The estimated costs were always high and, although money was there through the generosity of a previous incumbent, the Reverend Basil Pitt who left £90,000 to the church, some of this was used for other expenses of the chaplaincy and became partially eroded. In 2002, more had been used to carry out badly needed alterations to and maintenance of The Hermitage, the chaplain's grace-and-favour Girne residence. Early in 2003 therefore, Anthony Fletcher in his ebullient way set about raising £100,000, the sum estimated by the architect as necessary to complete the restoration. We were fortunate in many ways: St Andrew's was a listed building and very much under the protection of the government antiquities' department, but we were blessed with the services of Oz Feridun as our architect. Oz is married to the Minister for Antiquities, so the plans he produced were in harmony with the department's wishes and concerns. Also, this charming and generous man insisted that his services would be given free of charge, as his personal contribution to God's work in the British community.

Work had to begin with the demolition of the east wall and deep excavation of the ground beyond. The overall scheme was to replicate the original building as far as was possible, using old drawings and photographs. Because the old chancel had almost collapsed, its foundations were obviously suspect, and with reason. It was found that the ground was infill material deposited there by the Venetians when they fortified and extended Kyrenia castle, just opposite the church, and still unstable. At the same time, it was discovered that the main building itself was also in danger of following the chancel down the hill sometime within the next ten years or so. Recognising that the area would have to be excavated down to the original bedrock before re-building could be started, Anthony persuaded the architect that, rather than construct a massive concrete frame merely to support the new chancel, it would be better to use the space below to create a much-needed church hall almost for no extra cost. The final plans were approved by our Bishop in Nicosia, the church council and the Ministry of Antiquities and so work began, long before all the funds were in place.

For this courageous act of faith one must salute the confidence and determination of Anthony Fletcher in pushing for the project to go ahead regardless. Characteristically, Anthony was at the forefront of the campaign to collect the money, ably assisted by Hilton Moses, chairman of the restoration's financial committee, that Antony set up for the purpose. Interestingly, around 90% of the monies were collected from outside North Cyprus, with generous donations coming from other chaplaincies in South Cyprus and elsewhere in the larger Diocese of Cyprus and the Gulf. The so-called 'Friends of St Andrew's' contributed much also. This group is made up of visitors to the island and former holiday-makers who have worshipped at the church and who want to continue to help throughout the year.

The building work was carried out by Korman's, generally recognised as one of the best construction companies in the North. I found it rather moving to observe the Muslim labourers from the Turkish mainland as they paused in building a Christian Church in order to observe their own cycle of prayer which, for the believer, is five times a day. As the town's main mosque, situated in Kyrenia's harbour area, is barely a stone's throw away from the church, it was not difficult for them to hear the muezzin calling from the minaret. For those readers interested, the devout Muslim turns at prayer times to face the Ka'aba in Mecca, in general terms south-east of Cyprus, which houses the huge black meteorite said to be the remnant of the shrine given to Abraham by the angel Gabriel. Every Muslim is expected to make at least one pilgrimage to Mecca in his lifetime in order to take part in the annual ceremony of encircling the Ka'aba together with thousands of others. Elsewhere, the believer prostrates himself before Allah at Shorooq (sunrise), Zuhr (noon), Asr (mid-afternoon), Maghreb (sunset) and Isha (night). The times are carefully calculated in accordance with the moon's phases and with astronomical precision according to whereabouts in the world the Muslim is, so that as the globe turns there is a never-ending wave of prayer being offered to Allah.

Of necessity, St Andrew's was evacuated while the work progressed and we moved into temporary premises at the Cheshire Home on the outskirts of the town. The committee members of the Home, headed up by Dr Haluk Avni Akman, were very helpful to the congregation in their hour of need and made us most welcome by literally throwing open the whole building to us each Sunday. We were able to set out the 'church' with the articles we had brought from St Andrew's each Saturday morning, and put everything away again after Sunday services ready for the Home to take in its visiting patients on Monday.

The People's Warden, a stalwart Scot originally from Glasgow, undertook the onerous job of being the link man with the builders and all their contractors, This meant that Jim more or less lived at the church during its reconstruction, as various crises arose on an almost daily basis, but to his lasting credit Jim stuck stoically to the task and saw it through to its triumphant end. We were all fascinated to learn, when the final excavations for the new chancel were completed, how it became evident that a major contributor to the literal downfall of the original building was a drain or spring, thought to date from Roman times, trickling away under the ground and steadily eroding the foundations. This was diverted into a channel well away from the new building and ducted to the sea nearby. We were in the Cheshire Home for Sunday services for a little over ten months by which time Korman's had completed the work and the restored church was ready for its rededication service, conducted on 30th November 2003, St Andrew's day, by our Bishop, The Most Reverend Clive Handford. With all paid for by that time, there was still some £5,000 remaining for possible additions to the building such as central heating, or a generator to keep us going during the all-too-frequent power-cuts.

Coincidental with the completion of the church restoration and extension, the number of ex-pat Brits coming out here to live is increasing, chiefly those who have retired and, like Meryl and me, are seeking a more peaceful life in a warm and clean climate. Many of them are churchgoers, naturally, and it is as well that the restoration has given us seating for up to 140 worshippers within the church itself instead of the 70 formerly. A new sound system that covers the whole building means that we can use the church hall downstairs or the grounds outside in fine weather on special occasions or festivals when even this number is exceeded. (PLATE 15)

Shortly after the re-opening of St Andrew's, Anthony confided in me that he intended, with the Bishop's agreement, to apply for the job of Vicar of Lyneham in Wiltshire; ironically the place where he had been RAF chaplain prior to leaving the Service and coming to North Cyprus. Anthony felt that although he had no knowledge of the precise condition of St Andrew's fabric before he took up the post in Kyrenia, it became clear to him that it was God's Will for him to shoulder the burden of its restoration and extension. In the meantime, over the five years of Anthony's absence, RAF Lyneham began an extended period of shutdown that meant the church there being returned shortly to civilian use and coming again under the control of the Diocese of Salisbury. Needless to say, Anthony was appointed to the post and, with Jane, left the island in May 2004. For me, the wonderful restoration of St Andrew's and its extension will be a lasting memorial to Anthony and his great dedication to that task. In St Paul's, London, a plaque near to Sir Christopher Wren's tomb bears the legend, *SI MONUMENTUM REQUIRIS, CIRCUMSPICE* – if you seek his monument, look around. I think the same can be said of Anthony Fletcher in St Andrew's, Kyrenia.

In the interim period following the Fletchers' departure and the new chaplain and his wife arriving, we were provided with a series of *locum tenentes* by the Bishop, mostly retired clergy from Exeter Cathedral, the English Diocese with which we are linked. Two of them, Canon Ken Parry with his wife Barbara and Archdeacon Tony Trembath with his wife Pat, were great characters and full of amusing stories about their times in the Cathedral. Barbara once told me how as Canon Precentor, Ken was entitled to a grace-and-favour house in the Cathedral Close, information that turned me green with envy – until she explained how the Close was full of drunks, tramps, drug-addicts and general ne'er-do-wells more or less 24 hours a day. At all hours they could get knocks on their door aggressively demanding food or money for drugs. Barbara said the noise of their activities reverberated throughout the night and she would occasionally, in desperation, fling up their bedroom window and 'bawl like a fishwife' for them to go away or to be quiet. She and Ken couldn't wait to leave. Ah well, I thought, another dream shattered as I had always longed to live in a cathedral close, imagining only the occasional sound of bells and a deep, reverential silence withal. Tony's wife Pat, on the other hand, used to pull his leg about an 'Archdeacon' being known as 'the crook on the Bishop's staff', an old chestnut amongst clergy no doubt but new to those of us at St Andrew's.

Ken had stories of his own to relate. As Canon Precentor at Exeter for a time, that is, in charge of the cathedral's music, one of his duties was to preside over the selection of promising boys for the Choir School, and the lists of applicants were always over-subscribed for the number of places available. As part of their interview, each boy was asked to bring with him a suitable piece of music he was comfortable singing. The sheet would then be passed to the organist available on the day to accompany the lad. One particular aspirant, eight years old, handed his music to the principal organist of Exeter cathedral, an internationally-renowned player to concert standard, lecturer, examiner and teacher, fixed him with a baleful stare and said; 'I hope you can play it properly, because it's *very* difficult'.

Ken had another lovely story to amuse us. Being asked to join the anniversary party of an elderly couple celebrating no fewer than 60 years of marriage, he ventured to ask the wife whether in all that time, she had ever contemplated divorce. She was horrified and huffily replied, 'Never!' After a moment's thought, she added, 'Murder, yes!'

Even so, it was with feelings of great relief and joy that we welcomed the arrival of Tony Jeynes at the beginning of November 2004 as our permanent chaplain, together with his wife Irene. Tony has had over 35 years' experience as a parish priest in England, notably in the County of Lancashire. He and Irene saw the challenge of working abroad as a fitting end to his long and successful career of bringing the Gospel message to all. In the relatively short time Tony has been with us, his thoughtful and skilfully constructed sermons are listened to intently and stimulate serious thought and discussion amongst the congregation. He has a wonderful way too of lifting the spiritual value of each service to what seems to some a new plane. Tony has endeared himself not only to existing members of the church but has also attracted an increasing number of regular worshippers each Sunday – to the extent that I sometimes wonder whether another church extension might be needed before long! St Andrew's has also played host to many hundreds of holiday-makers over the years and it is pleasing to see how these numbers too are increasing under Tony's pastoral care.

Each year, usually in late January, the Diocese of Cyprus and the Gulf holds its annual Synod at an hotel in Larnaca, in the south of Cyprus. With the lifting of travel restrictions, members of St Andrew's were able to participate for the first time in early 2005. Consequently a party of six, including Tony and his wife Irene, made our way across the border and booked in at the Lordos Beach Hotel. Not knowing quite what to expect, we all found the event a fascinating and worthwhile experience.

In all, some 130 delegates and observers attended, with the greatest numbers coming from the seven chaplaincies on Cyprus. The agenda was lengthy, which meant the conference lasted over almost an entire working week, and there was plenty of work to be done. Many of the discussions revolved around the day-to-day activities of the various chaplaincies in the Gulf States and their financial affairs, as well as those on Cyprus itself, but one afternoon the Bishop introduced the Rev Canon Andrew White, who held us enthralled by his account of the situation at St George's, Baghdad. Andrew is officially a Canon at Coventry Cathedral but seconded to St George's. He told us harrowing tales of the difficulties of bringing the Gospel there under almost impossible conditions. The church survived heavy allied bombing attacks on two adjacent buildings, both important government offices of the regime of Saddam Hussein, but understandably it was affected by the blasts. Because of his work elsewhere, Andrew is not in residence all the time but returned to Baghdad shortly after the main fighting was over.

In the meantime, the building had been looted and further damaged by vandalism. Andrew had by no means lost his sense of humour and told us how the key to the locked St George's safe had been missing for years. The looters, not surprisingly having ready access to explosives, had blasted the safe open, removing anything they felt to be of value. Astonishingly, they had left the large and beautiful solid silver cross that normally stood on the high altar, so Andrew saw that as a positive benefit of the war. Andrew is clearly made of super-human material and, despite the appalling situation, set about restoring the building to a state where services could resume. The congregations were chiefly Chaldean and Assyrian Christians, with many of the US and UK armed services' personnel attending also. Sadly, after the recent events, most of the regular congregation are poor, with many widows and orphans, but there are some Muslims too who like to attend St George's.

To illustrate the atmosphere of his life in Baghdad, Andrew told us how his driver and bodyguards will not get into the car until they have watched him pray and then ask whether Andrew's 'personal angels' are there with them. Only on being thus reassured, will they begin often hazardous and, to us, terrifying journeys throughout Iraq. There is the serious danger of bullets and bombs as well as the ever present one of kidnap. Andrew held his audience spellbound for well over an hour, during which time the dropping of a pin would have been deafening. Whilst many of his stories were entertaining, others reduced some of us to tears.

One of the major issues before the World-wide Anglican Communion at that time was the Windsor Report, commissioned by the Archbishop of Canterbury, and concerning the election of Gene Robinson, a practising homosexual priest in the Episcopal Church of the USA, to the post of bishop, and the blessing of same-sex marriages in the Church of Canada, both groups being part of our Communion. Naturally, this is a very distressing trend and somewhat bitterly opposed by many members of the Communion, who see both as serious and unacceptable departures from the teachings of our religion and scripture. Decisions to make such radical changes have been taken without due reference to other members of the Communion, including the Archbishop of Canterbury. Bishop Clive had earlier asked each chaplaincy to consider the report, some 91 pages in length, debate the issues in their church councils and to send their findings to him before Synod met. From these documents, Bishop Clive produced a summary report that included references, comments and suggestions from the chaplaincies. Discussion and debate on Wednesday afternoon subsequently formed an important part of Synod, as Bishop Clive was to attend a meeting of the Primates, to be chaired by Archbishop Rowan Williams in Belfast at the end of February, and he wished to carry our views with him.

Happily, the rest of Synod was not as deep as this disturbing matter; on Tuesday, we spent the morning of our Quiet Day at a nearby Orthodox Monastery. The monks made us all most welcome, put the place at our disposal and supplied their delicious 'forest tea' and cool drinks while we listened to addresses from one of our guest speakers, Angela Ashwin. Angela has written several books on prayer and conducted many other addresses at various services held in the hotel throughout Synod. During periods of contemplation at the monastery, we wandered in the beautiful grounds with only the sound of birdsong and the cool, early spring breeze, soughing through the many lovely trees.

On Wednesday afternoon we were bussed over to St Barnabas' Church in Limassol, where Bishop Clive licensed two clergy for work in the Diocese. This particular service is known as the Synod Eucharist. Again, we were made most welcome and treated beforehand to a proper and delicious English tea produced by members of the congregation.

St Andrew's has its own resident characters too. Dottie, for example, I call one of North Cyprus's national treasures. She has the spare build of a sparrow, the serenity of Mother Teresa and, at the time of writing, she is 93. Now widowed, Dottie is on her own for most of the year but is joined regularly by her son 'Jay-Jay' who comes out from the UK to enjoy her company and vice-versa. Dottie lives up the hill on the road to Bellapais and settled there with her husband many years ago, long before the 1974 watershed, thus remembering the island in its more tranquil, less frenetic days. Dottie drives her car still with great panache – so much so that she gets the occasional speeding ticket. She bathes daily in the sea from May to October around 7 am, swimming by the castle on the outlying approaches to Kyrenia harbour. Despite this healthy activity, Dottie professes to feel the cold acutely and says her epitaph should read, 'She was last into cotton and first into wool'. Dottie is one of the readers at St Andrew's with a great knowledge of the Bible and a strong preference for the Old Testament, most of which, I suspect, she knows by heart. Amazingly – to me at any rate – she reads without spectacles. According to legend, Dottie was an actress and, with her beautifully modulated and mellifluous voice, it is easy enough to believe. She can effortlessly wring the slightest nuance and meaning from the most unlikely-looking text and bring it to vibrant life.

A few years ago, criminals from the UK would arrive clandestinely in North Cyprus under the impression they were free from arrest and repatriation to the UK for their crimes. In this respect, things have also changed and this is no longer a safe haven for villains. Some years back, then, one such middle-aged gentleman arrived and somehow befriended Dottie. He was completely unknown to other British residents at that time but was wanted back at home for drug-smuggling on an international scale. As unaware as the rest of us, Dottie was charmed by this man who was attentive, considerate and well-mannered towards her, taking her to lunch and sending her flowers. Villain or not, there must have been much to admire and respect in the man because Dottie is no fool. Inevitably, of course, the law began to catch up with him and he disappeared quite suddenly, and the facts about his past quickly became known. To our great amusement, we heard how

Jay-Jay wrote shortly afterwards to his brother, 'Do you realise that at 90' (as Dottie was then) 'our mother has become a gangster's moll?'.

In Kyrenia

North Cyprus banks are different too. Coming from the UK and finding oneself in need of a bank to make regular money transfers, it is something of a surprise to enter such a building and find not a full-height security wall of hard-wood, stainless-steel and armoured glass to cut off and protect the staff but a normal counter such as one might find in a draper's shop. In my own bank, the large, five-foot high steel safe at the rear of the banking area is unlocked when the bank opens, its door usually wide, sometimes with mountains of cash in all currencies on show to the customers and so it remains until the place shuts for the day. Visitors who wish to see the bank's manager simply walk around the side of the counter, past the safe and into his office through the ever-open door. Mostly they greet a member of staff or two who respond smilingly as the visitor progresses through the building. It's what I call 'relaxed banking' and seems to be standard procedure throughout the north.

However, there are perhaps some obvious reasons why this should be. First, the small population means that everyone knows who everyone else is. Many of us Brits think we go about unnoticed, but almost whenever I need to explain to a local where Meryl and I live, they already know not only the village but the exact location of the house, which can be scary as we think we're quite isolated on the edge of Ozanköy. Secondly, on this tiny part of the island there's nowhere easily to run if you're committing a felony and the police crime-detection rate must be relatively one of the highest in the world. It is extraordinary how quickly a suspect is picked up after a crime is reported; anything from handbag snatching (mercifully rare) to murder (even rarer!). Thirdly, I suppose, the police are armed and there are, after all, around forty thousand troops readily available as back-up. Altogether this adds up to a very risky prospect for the would-be bank-robber, and long may this happy state last.

Many ex-pats, for various reasons, such as gun and driving licences, immigration visas and other business, need to visit the police station in Girne fairly frequently during the year. Surprisingly to some readers perhaps, most of us find it a pleasure. One is always made to feel welcome and treated with the utmost courtesy. Many of the officers speak excellent English and are pleased usually to have an opportunity to exercise their language skills. Whenever there are Turkish forms to be filled, they are happy to help and one is usually invited to take coffee or tea with them while the meeting takes place. All these pleasantries go to make life very relaxed and satisfying for the ex-pat settled in a foreign land.

CHAPTER XIV
EPILOGUE

North and south Cyprus, at the time of writing, are changing rapidly – dynamically even, and literally overnight in some respects, so that much of the information in this book concerning general current affairs, politics, building development and the overall economies of both will inevitably have gone out of date. It is a certainty that Turkish Cypriots on the island and abroad pray fervently for a lasting solution to the 'Cyprus problem' after many years of frustration. Turkish Cypriots faced mortal danger at the beginning of the troubles, and deep uncertainty about their future following the intervention of 1974 from the Turkish mainland. Despite the recent acceptance of the 'whole geographical island' into the EU, the Turkish side refuses to accept that the 'Republic of Cyprus' represents them. I hope that some of the comments I have made in this book will help make clear why they do not.

Turkish and Turkish Cypriot Governments together remain determined to see a fair and just settlement between north and south but not at the expense of compromising all that has gone before. One thing is however certain: the hard-won freedom and peace that the Turkish Cypriots enjoy today will not be thrown away carelessly. They are fully entitled to play a full and proper part in governing the affairs of the island of Cyprus and to be treated as equal partners by the

Greek side. This is the fundamental premise of the Annan Plan. The refusal by the Greek Cypriots to recognise this right or to return to the negotiating table as urged by the European and World communities suggest that further serious difficulties lie ahead and it is vital that the Turkish side acts adroitly and avoids the countless traps set so regularly by the Greeks. Pressure generated world-wide by the Greek community and its propaganda machine is on Turkey at the moment to recognise the 'Republic of Cyprus' as a member state of the EU, whereupon Turkey would be automatically obliged to remove all its military from the island, the thirty-one-year-long objective of the Greek Cypriots, and to open its sea and airports to Greek Cypriot shipping and aircraft. To its credit, Turkey has made it clear they will do none of these things before a settlement on Cyprus is reached.

In the meantime many folk, having heard our story, ask Meryl and me whether we think we made the right decision. We always reply that although the Garden of Eden vanished long ago, of all the places there are to live on the planet, North Cyprus seems to us to be well up in the top few. Nothing remains unchanged for long, but taking the land as it is today, with its deep and venerable history, the friendly local people, the wonderful, healthy climate, the still-beautiful countryside and the relatively low cost of living it seems to us difficult to beat. If you are thinking seriously of living abroad, don't make the mistake of leaving North Cyprus off your list of places to be looked at very carefully. At the very least, do come and see it for yourself. But, remember that old saying of the locals: 'Once you've visited Cyprus, you'll come back...'

Ozanköy, December 2005

BIBLIOGRAPHY

Bitter Lemons, by Lawrence Durrell, first published by Faber and Faber, in 1957

Cyprus, by Sir Harry Luke, first published by George G Harrap & Co Ltd., in 1957

Eats, Shoots and Leaves, by Lynn Truss, first published by Profile Books Ltd., in 2003

Guide to North Cyprus, published by the TRNC Tourist Office, in 1989

Historic Cyprus, by Rupert Gunnis, first published in 1936

In the Steps of the Master, by HV Morton, first published by Rich and Cowan Ltd., in 1934

Journey into Cyprus, by Colin Thubron, first published by William Heinemann in 1975

Northern Cyprus, by Kristina Gursoy & Lavinia Neville Smith, first published by Landmark Guides in 2000

PLATE 1

PLATE 2

PLATE 3

PLATE 4

PLATE 5

PLATE 6

213

St Sophia Cathedral in Nicosia

PLATE 7

214

PLATE 8

PLATE 9

216

Queen's Window, St Hilarion

PLATE 10

217

Buffavento Castle

PLATE 11

218

Kantara Castle

PLATE 12

219

Neptune in Kyrenia Old Harbour

PLATE 13

A&M Villa and pool in Ozankoy

PLATE 14

St Andrew's Church

PLATE 15